The Blue Dress

The Blue Dress

Poems & Prose Poems

Alison Townsend

WHITE PINE PRESS • BUFFALO, NEW YORK

First Edition

Library of Congress Control Number: 2003100348

ISBN: 978-1-893996-61-8

Edited by Robert Alexander

Printed and bound in the United States of America

The Marie Alexander Poetry Series, Volume 6

The publication of *The Blue Dress* has been made possible by support from Robert
Alexander and with public funds from the New York State Council on the Arts, a State
Agency.

Cover Art: William McGregor Paxton (American, 1869–1941). *The Other Room*. Oil on
canvas. El Paso Museum of Art, purchased with funds raised by the Member's Guild
of the El Paso Museum of Art.

White Pine Press
P.O. Box 236
Buffalo, NY 14201

www.whitepine.org

Loss is the first step toward fullness.
—Octavio Paz

In memory of my mother, Mary Doak Townsend, 1919-1962,

for Holly Prado Northup and Susan Wicks,
friends of the soul,

and for Tom, for the future

Contents

II. Truth Serum

III. The Blue Dress

Lifeline

The woman is in love with the poem. It is a short poem, carved in the shape of a deer from ice. Its antlers are twigs coated with silver. Each hoofprint reflects movement, the light of changing stars. It is a poem of snow, a story flung like a fistful of winter across house, forest, field. But it is not a cold poem. Somewhere deep within the deer's body a small red berry quivers, names itself as heart.

The woman has dreamed the poem. It has come to her in the night, pulled while she sleeps, from the breath of her childhood. It has plunged and moved, galloping in a deer's body for many miles across snow-encrusted fields. The deer navigates by instinct, its head raised windward in search of home.

At rest now, stabled in her hands, the deer is very still. It is a statue that conveys its message in silence. The woman holds the deer close, until it melts returning, she does not know where, her own journey beginning with the return. There is red in her palms. Starlight and winter darkness. She does not know what to do with so much sacred water.

I.

Calf Season

Red: A Poem in Five Parts

I.

Out running, I notice Mount Baldy,
first snow of the season
shot crimson
in the long, slanting light.
Its color fills me
and I remember
you taught me the name for this,
saying it over and over
as if it was a password
floating between us, pure
as white flakes on a high mountain.
Alpenglow, was what you whispered.
When the sun hits the snow
on the side of the mountain
they call it alpenglow.

II.

This afternoon
I found blood on myself.
Simply my own blood,
an ordinary cycle,
but it could have been our blood,
what we have burned through together
and what returns, regular
as the tides of my own
body which have known your tides
as they know no others.

Washing my white pants
in the coldest water,
I felt a rose bloom,
fresh and eternal as a line
from the oldest story.
The story which says,
I don't care if it's all
been written before me.
The story which says,
What we do daily is begin again.

III.

Tonight,
passing the still yard
of the house where no one lives,
I saw a single leaf fall,
crescent-shaped and particular
as a small canoe skimming
into a pond of red.
I was the only one
to ever see it.
The only one to hear
the swish of its bright, dying cells
twirling through evening.
I have to tell him, I thought.
I have to tell him
of the story I seemed to hear
in that moment
about a man and a woman,

their lives spinning together
into the place
beyond surrender, the whole
street hushed and silent,
attentive while one leaf fell.

IV.

You brought me a leaf once, scarlet,
iced clear by a cold Texas rain.
You savored its outline in crystal,
telling me, *Look!*
Isn't it beautiful?
You knelt beside the bed,
holding it, saying,
It's the most beautiful
thing I have ever seen.
I looked, at the leaf
(which was lovely)
balanced like light
on the field of your mitten.
But it is your face I remember
when I think of the word *beautiful,*
holding it carefully balanced inside me
the way you held that leaf
in the middle of winter,
like an offering,
a small bonfire leaping
from your hand.

V.

And now, walking the thick
dark after my long run,
feeling the hot apples flare,
then hush, then flare into my cheeks again,
I glance up and see house lights
spreading themselves over the driveway
in a spill of gold and red.
I see house lights,
and your outline
printed across me
like the shape of something I have
always known but rarely named.
What it has taken me this long
to discover about passion,
about patience,
about simple forgiveness.
I glance up and see house lights
and the place where our lives
meet in a single color,
like that word you taught me
when we first met.
Alpenglow, alpenglow,
saying it over and over
as if it named us—
a field of snow on the side
of a mountain,
a shift of white
burning into red.

Baldy Notch, via Devil's Backbone

Once, climbing Mount Baldy in August, seven bighorn sheep crossed our path. Ghostly and gray, they rose out of steep scree to stand poised on the faint line that led to the top of the mountain. Breathless and hot in the thin air, we were emptied then opened by what we saw. Our hearts bolted and froze on our dry tongues, while we stared, mesmerized by their hypnotic yellow eyes with the unflinching pupils, their scrolled horns, their silent hooves.

It was a long moment, spilled like a lake on that razorback saddle. We looked into one another and beyond, into the real life of the mountain. Then the big male dipped his horns and the herd was gone, absorbed like air into the ridgeline as quietly as they had come. It could have been a dream, but it wasn't. And we continued the last mile to the bare peak that rose, spreading its granite skirt like a mantle of light to the desert.

We arrived, but to this day it's that sighting I remember. When I feel most far from you, I remind myself that you were the one standing beside me that hot noon, looking straight into wildness.

No Matter How Much Sunlight

We watched a program about depression last Friday, sitting together over pizza and beer. It wasn't about those blues we all get—aching scat-songs of frustrated desire—but about the real thing, illness opening its black rose in time-lapse, rank garden where the brain chemistry's gone bad.

The program didn't tell us anything I hadn't already discovered, groping my way through the fog those two years, tapping my fingers along earth's musty ceiling, searching for the combination that would release me into the meadow where I'd been standing the day the ground fell through.

It was the same old information—drugs, talk therapy, the electroconvulsive shock I'd once begged for, desperate for a cure. I watched, distant, critical, bored, demanding "more depth," words that could describe the mind as tar pit, moonscape, a smoldering slag heap where the world goes silent, empty of color as a 1920s film.

But afterwards I couldn't stop crying at how close that underworld still is, and how clearly I remember the taste of dirt in my mouth. And how the predilection for sadness is embedded within me, an obsidian arrow lodged in the heart, no matter how tight your good arms are around me, or how much sunlight I stand in, or how far I've traveled away from the dark.

Relapse

The Mourning Cloak butterfly
that flutters through the air in frantic circles,
a rope of spider silk clinging to her wings.
The chipmunk whose small sides go still,
even as I pry my tabby cat's jaws open.
The little boy in the waiting room
at the psychiatrist's office
who asks the receptionist *Where is Mommy?*
and is sent back to look at Spiderman and Hulk.
The broken shape I flinch from on the road
until I see it is a fallen branch, not
the cat or the doves I feed, my fear evaporating
as fast as the alcohol the lab tech swabs
my skin with before she draws my blood.
The young man who begins to cry in my office
because his father made him major in business
when all he really wants to do is write.
The words like flint I hurled at my husband
this morning. The words he hurled at me.
The corgi-beagle mutt who died the summer
I was twenty. The silk of her ears.
The men who've left me. The men I've left.
My mother dying of cancer when she promised
she'd return. The pink of Naked Lady lilies
wilting in the heat. The way the light slants,
its angle ever more aching and acute in August.
How everything passes through me as if
to perceive is to be perpetually permeable,
a fist of sadness tightening about the heart.

How there is nothing I can do about any of it
though I would do everything if I could.

How one cricket chirps,
as alone and out of place as I am in the hard
brightness of this weekday afternoon,
as we all are, caught like creatures in amber,
in the spell of our miraculous lives.

Daily

Each afternoon as I drive home from work,
accelerating hard where County P curves
outside Mt. Horeb, the spotted Percheron
stands in her triangular pasture,
poised at the edge of the woods.

She is always alone, cropping at something
under the snow, in a swath of sun so bright
it makes me look, then look again
at how she knows exactly the right moment
to turn her back to the wind.

I do not think she is unhappy,
here in her own field, curried by weather.
She is chestnut and white, and wears a halter,
which makes me think someone must love her.
But her coat stands up in tufts that catch

at the light and make a psalm of her body.
And her mane is like raw silk tangled with burdock.
Nothing but wind has touched her since morning.

Twelve Below Zero

Audubon says the red-breasted nuthatch
will accept suet, but is small and shy,
visiting bird feeders less frequently
than its white-breasted cousin.

But every day this week a pair has come
to our feeder, their underfeathers
rusty pink beneath serious blue-gray.
I know they mate for life.

This afternoon, out of sorts, washing
breakfast dishes in a rush to be finished,
I glanced out through steam and saw
Lake Mendota's frozen reaches blushing,

the trees on the far shore a scrim of smoky rose.
So many times this year I've thought of leaving.
I see it's red that makes me stay, the heart
going on about its intractable business

while small birds dart and flash,
their wings opening and closing
over the fat and the gold seed, like bellows
fanning winter into flame.

Spring Geography

Two days after my birthday, the first warm night. With the windows open the freeway comes closer, but so does the weather. In the bedroom I fold laundry by lamplight. My clothes. Your clothes. Clean sheets tumbled, green upon the bed.

In the next room you sit, riffling the pages of an atlas through your fingers like water. You are looking for "Whitefish," the name of a bay you heard mentioned as refuge-just-missed, tragically, in a '70's folk song. You want to place it, the way you place all things, in the realm of the rational, the shape of an indigo blue bay upon paper a real thing, something you can point to, measuring its distance with the length of one finger.

I do not know how to measure you. Holding an armful of warm towels, I come, stand quietly beside you. Together we look down like birds over a map of the Great Lakes. You've found the bay, carved like a face we both know into an otherwise treacherous shoreline. But it's the Lakes that excite us, those bodies of deep water. I ask if they freeze up in winter. You say you think so, in places, though they try to let ships pass, breaking ice to make a path through the middle.

I'm not sure you're right. And neither of us has been there, our opposite coastlines squeezing the middle into an invisible country where distance floats, clear but unspoken between us. There is so much we don't know. So much that maps never tell us. Why the ice breaks, for instance, cracking free on a large lake with a sound like gunpowder exploding. Why the weather has shifted. Why the light from this lamp moves me so, spilling in a gold circle over the marble top of my dresser.

I return to my work. The wind lifts my hair. It brings salt to my lips even forty miles from the ocean. *I couldn't live without the sea*, I said this afternoon. But I meant, *without mystery*, like whitecaps on the surface of dark water, sunlit for a moment before disappearing.

I spread the sheets on the bed. Printed with maidenhair, sword ferns, and swallowtails rising, they unfold with us, snowmelt watering the northernmost forest. I slip between these things, letting my nightgown fall like a flurry of snow or the ghost of a winter dream, dissolving there on the carpet below me. And then I call you, knowing, if only for now, that the truest geography lies here, warm, in the shape of our bodies that turn together like one needle knowing its compass.

You leave the atlas behind in the next room. In the window the curtain billows, white as a ship's sail scudding over open water beneath moonlight. The waves crash, circular, stinging. Beneath the cool sheets, we move closer together, setting out once again on this difficult journey, cutting a path across unknown waters that name us as we travel upon them, making up where we are as we go—shaken but persistent, rising and falling together, rising and falling, each one looking for refuge in the depths of this familiar, this forever unmappable bed.

Looking at MRI Scans of My Brain

My husband and I held the films up against the sliding glass door in Oregon the summer it seemed my sadness might never go away, trying to make sense of whatever illness swirled there in black and white and gray, so terrible the river winding through me seemed more real than I was, somewhere beneath the Douglas fir's shawl of liquid silver, the grape leaves unfurling their fuzz of green.

Here were thought and memory, feeling and dream. I stared into those transparent sheets of myself my husband traced with one finger as I'd seen him trace our route across a ten thousand foot mountain, following the convoluted folds and cross sections as patiently as he followed the slow lines of elevation.

And I thought, *This is what matters*—the transparent mind that lets the world through like a window, one we can open any time, whenever we want, the wind in our hair, mysterious, fern-delicate, human. Or is it his standing beside me that I remember, ready to remind me that what felt crazy was only a matter of degree, my footing on that mountain easily recovered by reaching my hand out to his as he balanced, just a few steps ahead, impossibly steady before me?

The Grief of Animals

All fall, as you prepared to leave us, pulling inside yourself like an imploding star, the black and gray-striped tabby, Blackberry, who'd chosen you when he was a kitten—bow-legged wriggle of silk you could hold in one palm—got sick, wheezing and choking with some odd feline asthma. Then sicker, vomiting two or three or four times a night, until it seemed everything torqued and twisted between us was reflected in those small flanks that heaved without relief, and the vet said, *Bring him in. I'm operating this morning.*

That day you waited two hours with him before surgery, patting his head steadily while you read *The New York Times.* And though I knew it was crazy I believed that if he made it, there was a chance we might. When I praised Blackberry's eyes, outlined perfectly in kohl, you praised mine until I couldn't see for the sadness. Later, I visited Blackberry and found you there before me, cradling him in your arms, an I.V. dangling from his paw until he could eat again and return home to patrol the yard, investigating what lies, half hidden, beneath new snow, while I learn solitude's difficult music.

And though I give him his pills, stroke his fur till it shines in stars of crackling static, and rub each vertebra in his long, flexible spine the way he likes it best—the way you used to when he jumped up on your chest every bedtime—I don't know how one eases the grief of a small animal who waits each day in the window beside the path where you walked home from work, his striped coat gleaming in the short light of winter.

In Any Language

I haven't spoken French for years.
But today old words find their way
back to my tongue:

je suis desolée;
j'ai beaucuop de tristesse;
je t'aime, je t'aime,

je t'aime. I haven't got the language
for the things I need to say,
just broken verbs, half-

remembered grammatical constructions
from high school where I first learned
to write of sadness with foreign words,

inscribing the lime-green covers
of my French *journal* with the names
of flowers—*muguet de bois,*

pensée, marguerites, tournesol.
Each one seemed something more than itself,
jumbled now as this garage I'm going through,

looking for a set of pressed glass dishes
embossed with *les fleurs* that we misplaced
two moves back, as if finding them

will answer my questions or summon
le mot juste for the shards I discover
everywhere, packed in boxes

or wrapped in bags we meant
to get back to, always
intending to mend

what might be unmendable.
We carried it all with us, shattered
but real, the way I carry these words

that have no place to return to,
floating on my tongue
like the bitter kisses

you pressed upon me,
walking away from me, then
walking back again, you

who had been
my lexicon of the body,
you who made language bloom again

like blood-red peonies in my brain.
The French for peony is *pivoine.*
And *sang* or blood is the scarlet thread

that pulsed, bright as speech, between us.
How empty of the right word for anything
my mouth has grown without you.

Red-Breasted Nuthatch

after the painting by John Wilde

The winter he left me I dreamed I was a bird. I shrugged my shoulders and I had wings. My hands snapped open, a pair of feathered fans married to the intricacies of air. It was more like swimming than flying, my legs scissoring the blue the way they'd once cut through the lake. Updrafts and downdrafts, lift and thrust and drag. Momentum was what propelled me from the gravity of loss, though a cross section of my wings would have revealed the shape of tears.

All winter my bird's body lifted me into places my woman's heart had feared. All winter my woman's body remembered how warm it once had been, until I saw that the broken parts of me had become one being. Bird and woman, woman and bird. Earth and sky and all the floating green islands of pine that dotted the landscape beneath me, every landmark a scribbled track of longing I followed, translating as accurately as one can translate the alphabet of birds.

Flight was what fed me. Flight was what kept me alive that winter, when earth was scorched with loss, when all the bones in my body filled with air and I bared even my breasts to the storm. When I walked outside in my nightgown, my feet went numb at 22 below. My wings were all that moved in that country.

Some nights, I can still feel cold burn through every shaft and barb of the feathered body I learned to call home that winter. *I was never there*, I tell myself, though I count how many wing beats it takes to cross the frozen lake. I have never left. And flight did not relinquish me, though I dream of it less now—as I contemplate the world through the nuthatch's bright and inscrutable eye.

The Habit of Its Fit

Love is made up of a great many things and I am not clever
enough to explain them. But I know that it is also habit.
———Jean Renoir

Ever since I took off my wedding ring
something floats around my finger
like the gravitational field of a new planet,
or an invisible cushion of air
that memory makes despite me.

My other fingers splay slightly apart,
still accommodating the shape of the wide
silver band engraved with leaves
that are half sea and half forest.
Absence becomes presence,

insistent as the thing itself,
and I arrange my life around emptiness
the way I once arranged it around
yours, struggling to fit even
when the fit cinched me, like a maple I saw

girdled by an iron ring but still growing.
One of my friends says, *Buy yourself a new ring,*
one of your own. She promises a "friendship band"
with my birthstone, like those we traded as girls.
But I think it takes the body a long time

to forget sixteen years with another,
to learn solitude—and the shape the soul
assumes alone, lying down on spring nights
in a white cotton nightgown like a girl
who has never been touched by a man,

but with the knowledge of a woman intent
on loneliness—that ghost-ring
spiraling around my finger like bands
of dust and light, the habit of its fit
reminding me how stubbornly wedded I am.

Instinct

When I saw the way the mother moose stood for days beside her dead calf, licking at it, nuzzling the still form that had already begun to decay —its coat tattered as worm-eaten velvet—as if her presence could make it rise again, stalks of legs unfolding beneath it like lengths of burnished sapling birch, the film disappearing from its eyes the way fog burns off a pond in midsummer, I understood how it was that I had waited beside you, everything I knew of devotion concentrated, each breath a slipknot of pain.

I saw that it was my task to stand guard, pawing the ground, shaking my head at intruders, impelled by the kind of crazy logic we call *constancy*, or *faith*, to remain close to what I'd loved, protecting it, keeping it away from the white teeth of the wolves that circled the place where you'd fallen—until I saw that it was me or you, and I left, crashing through the brush of my own life and into the clearing of who I might be without you.

Leaving Dorland Mountain

I have before seen other countries, in the same manner, give
themselves to you when you are about to leave them, but I had
forgotten what it meant.

—Isak Dinesen

On the last night,
when I do not dare to hope
that I might see them again,
they come to me, the beautiful
mother and her long-legged daughter,
drifting into the clearing
in coats of tawny smoke.
When I put my book down,
blow the final lamp out and pad
barefoot through the kitchen
for a glass of cold water,
I see them, lying down together
on the rough grass outside
my window, like two dreams
kneeling on a carpet
of finely woven light.

The moon is everywhere.
Almost full on this warm night,
rising above oak trees in a brief
swell of abandon before autumn,
she shows them to me
—what I have seen by day
but must meet in another

way before leaving—
this pair who browse there
beside me with no other purpose
but pleasure, moon-bathing
and waiting among the chirr
of crickets and hoots
of the horned owl,
resting, but not asleep.

They're so close I can see
their flanks moving, each breath
rippling like water beneath their ribs.
I can see their ears, translucent
as furred shells, flicking at sounds
I do not notice, and feel their gaze,
lambent as the moon itself,
turned deeply upon me
until the window melts
and there is nothing between us
but breathing measured
by the night's slow pulse.

The forest heaves
within my body, completely herself
in the guise of these lithe,
delicate women who come to say
that she will take me.
The reward for silence
and attention is acceptance.
The moon will do the rest.

And as I watch, the doe
begins to lick her daughter's face
softly, so softly I can almost
feel her tongue caress
my pale cheek into
russet velvet layered
over wands of slender bone.
All I want to do
is lie down there beside them,
slipping free of this tight skin
and letting that wild mother
lick me and tongue me and
polish me into a new life,
glistening and raw
as any naked creature
brought to birth from darkness
and baptized by the moon.

I want to go out there.
But because I want to keep them
this way, because the sound of my
foot on a loose board alarms them,
because I've been permitted
entrance into a secret world, I don't.

I just stand here, for a long time,
drinking cold water
and watching, while the deer
watch beside me.

The forest holds me.
In the hushed, nearly imperceptible
pause that comes between each breath
I am her own daughter,
innocent again and holy.

I have never felt so safe.

A Bowl of Sugar

Tonight I prepare apples the way my mother once made them, slender wedges with a bowl of sugar beside them for dipping, grains of glitter clinging, the thinnest line of sweetness sparkling along the outer edge. I don't know why I crave this confection this evening, or why the treat returns each year like the names of apples I ate when I was young— Winesap, Cortland, Northern Spy—except that it makes me a daughter once again in her absence,

as if she stands in the kitchen beside me, knife flashing, quick as my own long fingers that have grown so much like hers, slicing these near-translucent wafers I take between my lips, letting the grains of sugar dissolve in me slowly, melting against the wet-suede of my tongue. Then I swallow and am alone again, the last crickets stitching their music across a cloth of dark that is also sweet and unknown to me, familiar as sugar, as the girl still standing somewhere inside me, watching to see how it's done.

From One Life to the Next

All morning I've been raking leaves, scraping gunk from the gutters, dipping my fingers through the froth that floats on top, down to the rich, black muck underneath where oak and maple break down, no longer themselves but not yet earth, changing already from one life to the next.

As I am, I think, *in this third fall since he left.* And then stop, not wanting to define what I'm doing by absence, though all the familiar gestures ask me to—rake in my hand and kitchen spoon I'm using to dig with, other autumns flicking past like those old movies where calendar pages flash by, fluttering like leaves to indicate time passing.

Wind lifts the leaves. Even as I empty these gutters, pine needles settle inside them, flecks of dry gold sticking to the wet. So much of life is about clearing a small space, only to watch it fill again with leaves, lovers, branches—every departure a form of return.

This morning, half-dressed, interrupting one task for another, I knelt on the floor in my study, reading a book by a man I know slightly. I skipped to the last poem first, cheating a little to see how the story ended. It was a love poem, of course. For his wife, killed last winter in an accident on Cape Cod.

And I thought of how we couldn't live if we knew what lay before us, our sorrows and losses raked up into piles like leaves we burn or haul to the roadside or leave exactly where they are. Or these seasons that keep teaching us what persists. Or this simple black stuff I hold in my hand, humus, halfway to dirt—a substance my scientist father said was alive, explaining that soil breathes as it changes.

So that ever since, I have touched it more gently, remembering his words and how I once saw my grandfather in our garden, crumbling earth between his fingers so lovingly I felt I shouldn't look. But I did. As I do now, my palms inscribed with grit, my nails grubby, my skin dirt-stained, pungent as this yard but ready for winter, clear as the gutters on the roof of this old house where I sit, suddenly aware that I am happy.

Ordering Clothes from Victoria's Secret

No matter what I do,
I'll never look like these women.
No matter how many miles I run,
or how much yogurt I eat,
I'll never pour my body into its skin
the way these women are poured
into sun-bronzed breast and thigh,
their waists slender as my grandmother's
before she married.

Yet I order, choosing the "classic
cotton lycra leggings" in purple,
because my legs are stronger now
than they were when I was twenty;
the "provocative, body-seamed black dress
with the sweetheart neckline,"
because the hollow in my throat
my mother swore signifies beauty
has deepened over time;
and the "romantic floral knit dress
which buttons from its scooped neck
through a fitted bodice to the hem
of its midcalf length skirt,"
because the style is more alluring
than all the minis in the world.

I order
because it is my forty-fifth spring
and good to run in purple leggings,

my 36-A breasts riding high;
because the face that history
is inscribing becomes more my own each day;
because I wear the same size
I did at eighteen, my smile as wide
and bright as the day I got my braces off;
and because I remember the swath of auburn
that burned beneath the white
at my grandmother's nape,
like a hidden river
or a bright fire
after ten children and sixty years,
when my grandfather
stood behind her at her dressing table
and pulled the tortoise-shell pins,
one by one, softly, from her hair.

My Ex-Husband Asks Me Who Reads My Rough Drafts

No one, I say, over Thanksgiving dinner at the Fess, the rhinestone earrings I bought to please my lover brushing my cheeks like cool, knowledgeable fingers. Then I amend that to: *Well, my writing group does, of course. But mostly I read my own rough drafts now.* I don't know why he's asking or what it matters, the two of us poised at opposite sides of the table, polite and wary, but still family of a kind, thrown together this holiday by circumstances too complicated to question.

Dinner arrives, with all the trimmings, and we talk of other things. His job and mine. Econometric models for utility companies. The business of selling books for a living. He wears the navy blue sweater with a snowflake design that I helped him pick out at Brooks Brothers. I wear a bargain, teal-green silk from Shopko that he's never seen, the weird alchemy of divorce making strange what was once most familiar.

Pumpkin pie comes, followed by decaf—sweetened, with lots of extra cream—and all the silly things we know about one another float, unspoken, in the lamplight between us. We do not talk of the future.

But as he bends to sign his half of the check, I see again how he bent at our kitchen table, going over my manuscripts, pencil in hand, teaching himself about poetry because he loved me. And how it is for love's sake, and because no one in our lives can ever really be replaced, that he asks me this question I do not know how to answer, except with the words of this poem, this rough draft I am still in the process of revising.

Pouring

All week it's rained in California. All month it's rained, the coast battered and beaten, hillsides sliding toward the sea, solid ground suddenly gone, moving, changed. I know it all so well I don't even have to close my eyes to see it. Know it as if it were my own body or dream. And it is. *It's the closest thing I have to home,* I said to someone at work this morning, the hillsides in California misted green in January as they are nowhere else in the country. Spring at the wrong time of the year.

But it became so right when I lived there. California and what became my own. What became my family as surely as golden poppies and lupine and owl's clover bloom in the desert after the rain that changes everything. Which is why a part of me weeps, inconsolable still, an endless winter rainstorm pounding from within, no matter how far I go with my good, my growing, my reinvented life.

And so, of course, I call. Out of a sense of what? Responsibility? Allegiance? Concern? I call to make certain your family is safe. Your mom at the beach. Your dad in the Berkeley hills. Your sister at Point Reyes, that island in time, moving infinitesimally northward even as I dial the number I must now pause to remember. I call. As you called me at almost this same time last year, your voice shaky, telling me about the L.A. earthquake, what was home binding us together no matter how far we travel.

And I was glad you called. And you are glad I've called. And even as we speak it rains, and you remember aloud the year Mount Baldy got one hundred inches of precipitation. *One hundred inches!* you exclaim, as if it were a key to all we cannot say, the rain and snow, the facts of weather accumulating like mute measurements of the heart's extremes.

And there is a snow-capped mountain inside us and between us. And there is the ocean, and the storms coming in off the water, and the rise and fall of surf. And I see that even apart, even in our other and separate lives, we are writing a love poem to what crumbles and moves in the rain. To what grew and keeps growing in that desert made paradise, in the brown made green, in the land that changes and changes and changes . . . until we too are changed.

Epilogue

The past isn't over; it's not even past.
—William Faulkner

Because I'm moving from the house where we lived when we were married, and because I want to mark exactly the spot where we buried each cat, I call and ask you to come and help me remember. You come, of course. As I know you will. As you always do. But I'm not prepared for the sight of you at the front door, your thin face thinner, your dark blond hair threaded with more gray than I thought you'd ever have, infinitely strange and infinitely familiar.

And you are not prepared for me. *Squaw Valley?* you ask, reading the words on my purple sweatshirt, as if wondering what I could possibly have done there without you, high in those mountains you introduced me to, that snowy range, those Sierras that were always ours together, hiking or skiing, the bright air sluicing into our lungs. How many miles did I cover, walking beside you, the scuffed boots you gave me in 1976 still the ones I wear?

We chat, though I am so busy watching you that I instantly forget what we're talking about, noticing only how your hands shake. I rub my tea mug against my palm until I hear a small clinking and catch you looking at my new gold band.

Outside, we walk to the copse of white pine where we buried three cats, one in each season but spring. You returned each time to dig the grave and weep with me. I recall the places exactly, it turns out, but know also it is important to do this together, the small bones that lie beneath us our family when we were young.

In the house I show you the stone carver's sketch. Nothing mawkish, but something flat—a paving stone really—inscribed with each cat's name and date. I place it on the table before you. You look at the page, framing it with both hands, leaning into the wood as if you need it to hold you up. You look and look but do not speak, though I wish you would. Only later will I wish I'd touched your hand.

When it's time to go, you linger, tell me you remember repairing the rungs on the dining room chairs I still use. I give you the last few things of yours I've found, cleaning out closets. You tell me of your trip to Europe—a summer vacation, tracing the route your new wife's father took through the Alps in the war. I mention my father, D-Day, though I don't know exactly where he was.

They have all that stuff mapped, you say. And they probably do. But I don't know anymore what lies unmapped in the past, or how it becomes the history our lives make as they connect to other people. *I should let you go,* you say, when the phone rings. But you pause there in what was once the door to our house, waiting for something.

As I wait too, though there are no words to describe this sadness that hangs between us, folded and refolded as those topographical maps you used to consult when we hiked, measuring the contour lines with a thumbnail as familiar as my own, saying, *It's not far now. A few miles and we're home.*

Calf Season

Halfway between Mineral Point and Platteville
I see her standing alone in a field, all
that breaks the border between prairie and sky.

I don't know why I look, the sight
of one more Holstein in Wisconsin
as unremarkable as Monday or my rush

to get to work. But then she bends her head,
tonguing the bundle of wet black and white
at her feet, nuzzling it a little further

into the shock of air, and I see the afterbirth
trailing streamers of bloody silk behind her.
In a few minutes she will take care of this.

But now all she knows is to wash
the calf clean of its slick red bed,
pushing it up on delicate stilts of legs

until it stands by itself, glossy
as the morning light that licks us all
toward the next turning. I know it is always

the first day for someone, but I do not know why
I have been granted the privilege of this sight,
as I hurtle west on the highway, almost at the halfway

point in my life, washed into myself again
the way the calf is by her mother—by this rough,
this loving, this inevitable tongue of the world.

My Grandmother's Roses

In memory of Elizabeth Conway Doak, 1886–1982

Late in her life, when her vision was fading, and arthritis restricted her movements to a single upstairs room, my grandmother and I corresponded about roses. I lived in California then, a continent away from the great stone house in Philadelphia where she'd lived for sixty years. But the roses in my sunbaked yard seemed familiar and eased my ache for green, so I included descriptions in letters: a red climber that looked like a flamenco dancer, a pinkish floribunda that opened in a swirl, and the ivory beauty that grew outside my study, its petals like tissue edged with flame.

That sounds like Blaze, she wrote back about the red one, *or Dusky Maiden. The pink is surely Escapade. And the white one? Well, that could be Iceberg, Summer Snow, or even French Lace; it's hard to say without seeing.* Then she apologized for her handwriting, saying, *My eyes have left me, darling.*

She knew the history of each rose and informed me about its fragrance, winter hardiness, and resistance to disease, though she added, *This might, of course, vary without a real winter.* And then wrote of the riotous tumble that filled her whole side yard, and how she walked there, summer mornings, choosing roses for the hall, the sideboard, and her own room—where she dried petals in willow baskets, turning them daily until they were rustling scraps, ready to sprinkle with lavender deep in the folds of her linen.

The last time I saw her alive, there were rose petals drying in the library downstairs, the willow baskets piled high with bits of pink and white and red I glimpsed before I left the house—in a hurry, as I always was back then—not knowing what I saw or what it would have meant to stand before them, running my fingers through petals as sweet and musky as the cheek I had just kissed. The answers to all the questions I might have asked but didn't hung suspended there between us, like the half-decipherable line in her last letter: *May you grow to love roses as much as I do.*

II.

Truth Serum

Ring-O-Levio

Muggy summer evenings between supper and bed,
Bellewood Avenue hums with hordes of bored kids
waiting for darkness like something important,
our hands and faces sticky with ice cream
from the Good Humor Man or Bungalow Bar,
after which girls chant, *Bungalow Bar tastes like tar!*
The more you eat it, the sicker you are! laughing so hard
the Popsicles and Eskimo Pies rise back up in our throats.
The boys chuck jackknives, fart with their armpits,
dart in front of cars until we all begin to crackle and burn
with excitement, spitting sparks like a line of gunpowder dots

in a cap gun, and Bobby LaRousse
—who greases his hair back like Ice in *West Side Story*—
and the Irish kid from the next street over
—who I know by his sweaty baseball jersey smell—
choose teams: *You with the braids, you're on my side.*

Everything happens fast. The night sky glows
like the starry backdrop behind the school stage.
My team confetties through the neighborhood.
Kathy and I squish into her too-obvious storm cellar
and are dragged back screaming as prisoners
to her brother's Davy Crockett fort
where Jay Dickey, the biggest bully on the block
but too fat to run fast, guards us like stolen gold.
Only someone from your own team can free you.
Or free me, as I huddle with Kathy
in the musty dark, snapping Blackjack gum

and waiting to be rescued
by the Irish kid, as it turns out,
who swoops down past the guard, gets
both feet into the den, and shouts *Ring-o-levio!*
Ring-o-levio! grabbing my hand so hard I wince.
And everything since seems the same process
of capture and release, the little doors
of the heart opening and closing
as abruptly as those of the fort
that is a cave that is childhood

that is the Irish kid telling me, *You run good,*
for a girl. I almost say *well* but don't.
And already it is beginning,
though I am ten and he is twelve
and we do not know enough to touch;
we do not know enough to do anything
but crouch there together
in the prickly protection
of the blackberry bramble,
the calls of *Caught! Caught! Caught!*
echoing behind like the first
small sounds of August rain sifting
through the branches around us.

The Barbie Birthday

Girls learn how to be women not from their dolls but from the women around them.

—Yona Zeldis McDonough,

The first gift my father's girlfriend gave me was the Barbie I wanted. Not the original—blonde, pony-tailed Barbie in her zebra-striped swimsuit and matching cat-eye shades—but a bubble-cut brunette, her hair a color the box described as "Titian," a brownish-orange I've never seen since. But I didn't care. My hair was brown too. And Barbie was Barbie, the same impossible body when you stripped off her suit, peeling it down over those breasts without nipples, then pulling it back up again. Which was the whole point, of course.

There must have been a cake. And ten candles. And singing. But what I remember is how my future stepmother stepped from the car and into the house, her auburn curls bouncing in the early May light, her suit of fuchsia wool blooming like some exotic flower. Just that, then Barbie— whom I crept away with afterwards, stealing upstairs to play beneath a sunny window in what had been my parents' bedroom.

She likes me, she really likes me, I thought, recalling Shirley's smile when I opened the package. As I lifted the lid of Barbie's narrow, coffin-like box, she stared up at me, sloe-eyed, lids bruised blue, lashes caked thick with mascara, her mouth stuck in a pout both seductive and sullen. Alone, I turned her over and over in my hands, marveling at her stiff, shiny body—the torpedo breasts, the wasp waist, the tall-drink-of-water legs that didn't bend, and the feet on perpetual tiptoe, their arches crimped to fit her spike-heeled mules as she strutted across the sunny windowsill.

All Barbie had to do was glance back once and I followed, casting my lot with every girl on every block in America, signing on for life. She was who I wanted to be, though I couldn't have said that then, anymore than I could have said that Barbie was sex without sex. I don't think my step-mother-to-be knew that either, just that she wanted to please me, the eldest daughter who remembered too much and who had been too shy to visit. My mother had been dead five months, both her breasts cut off like raw meat. But I yearned for the doll she'd forbidden, as if Barbie could tell me what everything meant—how to be a woman when I was a girl with no mother, how to dress and talk, how to thank Shirley for the hard, plastic body that grew warm when I touched it, leading me back to the world.

With Monsters, 1964

Until my father remarried, a scant six months after my mother's death, I'd barely seen TV, my nose buried in books from the Philadelphia Free Library, my viewing rationed to *Lassie, Zorro,* and *The Wonderful World of Walt Disney* before it was even in color. But then my stepbrothers came. And with them came monsters. Wolfman, Dracula, Frankenstein and the Mummy tore into our living room as if they had always lived there.

I recognized myself in them—girl with the bad home-Toni perm and chipped front teeth who barely slept for fear they would get me and carry me off to the underworld where I thought I belonged—no way to quell the terror of being alive when my mother was not. They watched while I set the table for dinner, flipped Beatles cards with my sister, wept over the new math not even my father was smart enough to solve.

As soon as night came I was theirs, clasped in the formaldehyde reek of Frankenstein's arms or the stink of the Mummy, my neck bared to Dracula, fur sprouting from my skin as I scratched myself raw, not knowing it was the dead calling out to me as the dead do when left alone too soon. Or that monsters were the only thing ugly and big enough to prove I was crazy, everything turned into something other than what it was that raged through the darkness, fueled by primitive need and washed in the unearthly blue glow of our Zenith, commercials for Juicy Fruit or Tiger Paws or Vegematic all that tethered me to the house,

though my parents kept saying there was *nothing there.* I was letting my imagination *run wild*—girl who couldn't control herself, and wouldn't keep quiet about it—the whole family's wildness trapped inside my body, like an itch no one but me could scratch, as the monsters came for me again and again, the long, red welts I raised on my arms and legs the only sign they'd been there.

Truth Serum

The psychiatrist had a doll house and other toys in his office. But I never saw another child, only adults who came and went, their eyes averted over terrible secrets. I thought to myself, *This must be what it means to be crazy*, and cast my eyes down too, afraid I might catch it and get worse, or even be taken to Wingdale.

The vampire who lived outside my bedroom window came closer then, and the woods behind our house opened like the grave I believed my mother was trying to claw her way out of. But I didn't tell the doctor this when he slid open his desk drawer and offered me candy. I didn't tell him anything, convinced that the Tootsie Rolls, Dots, Jujubes and Star-Bursts contained a magic drug to make me talk, "truth" spilling from me in a sugary flood.

I didn't even know what "truth" was, but it was all I had, my mouth watering as I stared into the desk drawer, then turned away slowly, busying my hands, building a model horse while he watched me in silence.

All that winter I fitted the pieces together, gluing the body, currying the fuzzy sides, brushing the synthetic mane and tail with my fingers till the fake hair smelled sweaty and warm as the real thing. I named the horse "Chestnut Hill" after the bay gelding my mother had given me lessons to ride on, and galloped away on his back whenever Dr. Goodman took emergency phone calls from women threatening to swallow his pills.

"Throw them all out," he'd soothe the anonymous voice on the other end, while I gave Chestnut free rein. "Flush them right down the toilet." We leapt fence after stone fence until he hung up, and scribbled down a message—Librium—on a square of white paper. "This medicine will make you better," he told me. "Be sure and give this prescription to your dad." I nodded, cradling Chestnut's hard body and leatherette reins in my arms, the only things that could possibly save me.

And before I left his office he'd offer me sweets again, pulling open the desk drawer to display his sugary cache. And every time I refused, truth caught in my throat like a pebble, or a pill, or a piece of splintered rock candy I could neither spit out nor swallow.

Librium

Sometimes it comes back to me,
that synthetic sleep they forced on me
the winter I was ten,
nights as I lower myself
down the long black ladder
to where the last rungs
sway and dissolve into darkness,
and I see my mother leave for the hospital again,
the doorway of our house framing her body
like black borders around funeral announcements.
This will make you less afraid,
my father says as he hands me the capsule.
Half yellow, half green,
it is pretty in its own way, innocent
and unpresuming as pastel Easter candy.

I don't really believe what my father says.
But my stepmother waits at the front door,
her perfectly filed nails tapping the brass knob
I've begged them not to turn.
It's better this way, my father says.
And besides, nothing will happen to us.
You know we'll be back soon.

He is wrong.
People don't come back.
Anything can happen
when a door opens on darkness
then slams shut, death or worse clicking
like an emergency in the latch.

But I take the pill, still warm
from my father's hand, and swallow it quickly,
a good child, dispatching trouble
with a gulp of chocolate milk.
Then I go down, alone, to the place
where sleep drops its curtain
of brocade and black velvet.
And there is nothing—

nothing to be afraid of
or to remember, or to forget,
the dream-swirl of all
I cannot tell them pressing
just behind my lips.

My Life as a Horse

There was a time, before breasts,
before blood flowed, before boys' bodies
made me too aware, when I was a horse,
a shiny black filly with a lilt to her gallop,
dressed in a blaze and two pairs
of white stockings.

My friends Kathy and Nan
were horses too, and we vaulted
over stone walls together, our manes
floating like silk in the breeze.

We straddled branches, urged ourselves on
with whips of peeled willow,
neighed and pawed at the macadam
with hooves that rang like iron.
We were clover thunder together.
We were stampeding magic.
We were sweaty creatures
no one could understand.

Then my friends got real horses
and didn't need to play, occupied
by gymkhanas, the North Salem Hunt Club,
and the beautiful palomino and bay
whose muzzles felt soft as down
against my cheek when I nickered to them
in the tongue of our ancestor, Eohippus.

I carried on alone for a while,
galloping down Keeler Lane to the school bus,
whinnying at horses confined in their paddocks,
tossing my tangled braids fiercely,
until it got too hard by myself
and the ways of horses dissolved
like the first bloodstains
I washed from my jeans in cold water.

I was a girl. I wore a Teencharm bra, and boys
were suddenly the only things that mattered.
But sometimes, when I am out running,
or see a horse alone, she comes back to me,
that long gallop of rippling muscle,
that pretty filly, that girlhorse,
so silky and so unencumbered
by the laws of the body.

Magic 8

My father gave it to my sister
for her ninth birthday.
But sometimes, when no one
was around I'd slip
into her room and ask
the Magic 8 questions,
tilting the black ball
back and forth in my hands
until an answer floated into
the porthole window at the top,
white words on a blue triangle,
rising from depths as black
as the Faber-Castell ink
we used in eighth-grade art.

The box it came in said
the ball was *to be used*
for entertainment purposes only.
But it was designed to answer
yes-and-no questions,
and so I asked them all,
admitting my secret hopes
as confidentially as I imagined
Catholic kids did at confession.
And the oracle obliged,
responses swimming into focus
at my every request, though they
were never quite what I wanted
as I looked everywhere for signs

that I was normal, hoping
the ball would give me
answers like *It is certain*
or *All signs point to yes.*

No matter what I asked
the Magic 8 answered.
Would Bruce Colley
ask me to go steady?
Ask again later.
Would I really be grounded
the rest of the month?
It is decidedly so.
Might my parents give me
my own phone for Christmas?
My sources say no.

I always ran out of questions
and finally just sat there,
turning the ball over
and over in my hands as if
it was the witch's crystal
from *The Wizard of Oz,*
and I could see somewhere
far ahead in the future,
tiny figures full
of meaning running
toward me in the glass.

And still the answers
floated up, responding
as if by honest magic

to what I couldn't ask—
why my mother died young,
why my father remarried fast,
why looking out
my attic bedroom window
filled me with sadness—
as if the black ball
really knew more than I did,
stupid toy blinking open
and shut like an eye
that saw everything
and knew what life
was really about,
condensing it to one
of the twenty possible answers:

Reply hazy.
Cannot predict now.
Concentrate and try again.

Joan of Arc

I loved the story
about how they found Joan's heart
in the fire afterwards,
still throbbing, too pure to burn.

Of course I wanted to be like her,
pinned flat on my back in bed
by the stupefying heat
of my attic room in mid-summer,
the book about her life
held straight up above me,
rising toward the ceiling
like an indifferent angel.

I was twelve and yearned
to hear voices whisper from a tree
in a blur of liquid gold,
or to see the three saints
glowing on the path before me
in the form of miraculous children
who would describe my task so well
I knew no one else could do it.

The only voices I heard
were those of my father and stepmother
arguing downstairs through the wall
they had erected between them.

But there was always the armor.
I itched to try on the tunic
of glittering mail or the metal suit—
like the medieval ones I'd seen
at the Philadelphia Museum,
only a few inches taller than me.
I wanted to leap to obey
some divine instruction,

or agree to be a martyr,
purpose pressing its weight
firmly into my shoulder
as the shimmering voices
told me what to do next.

Even the stake
seemed glorious, a perfect
consummation of belief.

It's the heart that matters most.
But I didn't know any way
to stop my parents' voices
from hammering into mine.

And so I read on, wishing
I was French or at least Catholic,
rearranging Joan's story
as my own, so that even there
in the hot spaces that hung
like fiery tapestries
between my parents' words,
there was room for the holy,

for the purifying fire
that smoldered inside me,
as I put on the armor I'd pounded out
on the blazing anvil of family
until it fit like my own skin,
and I was burning up inside,

an ordinary girl
who had to go downstairs
and prepare supper
for her whole family,
nothing but the imagination
between her and the world.

Hunt Mountain

In memory of Michael Wittreich, 1951-2001

When the night my stepbrother put his wrists through the window became the summer we had to hide all the sharp objects in the house—knives with their glittering edges, razors, glass which could be shattered, ready to cut—we kids took to walking the mountain. Each evening after supper when fireflies kindled the air like sparks of cool lightning, we met, without plan, at the foot of the driveway, the white gate open on the road before us, the blue pines bleeding slowly into dusk.

Purposeless at first, sauntering past the neighbors', we moved slowly together, drifting along in August's inertia. Past the house, where Mr. Ranier stood, dour in gray farmer's clothing, his wife motionless on the porch swing beside him. Past the crazy Mahoneys'. Past Miss Keeler's, landlady and local patron of the arts, where twin pugs barked frantically behind a picket fence. Past it all we strode, away from our own home, leaving behind the place where my father sat brooding—pipe smoke wreathing the patio—and my stepmother's rage sizzled, sucking air from each room until breath itself felt like glass breaking.

Bickering, trading insults over our shoulders, we filled the air with conspiratorial humming until someone—maybe my stepbrother—said, *Let's go somewhere! Let's go somewhere now!* while Holsteins paused alongside in the meadow, listened, then lowered their heads to the grass. We picked up speed as we left house lights behind us. The road turned from black-top to hardscrabble under our sneakers. We walked fast, the Queen Anne's lace high as our shoulders, the ordinary world of stone walls and upland meadows another country dreaming itself into being. Blackberries gleamed. A fox yipped an inscrutable love song. Mountain laurel lifted bundles of white fire to the sky. My stepbrother led. We followed, panting, the road a dirt lane that pulled us upward to the sandy patch marked for picnics and parking.

We never stayed at the top long—there was nothing to do there—but crashed through the tangle of sumac and wild grape to a flat rock, our secret lookout over the curve of the valley. Far below lay the farms, studding the fields like fires set against night's arrival; the Titicus River, silver and slow in the marshlands; and our own house, grown minute and diminished. We felt so small, looking down on the lights. Home seemed so distant that we looked at one another and without a word began running, the real reason for climbing the mountain the pleasure of our descent.

Plunging from forest to field, we ran, sometimes paired, sometimes singly, crazed with momentum and the heat of our bodies, each one a boomerang arcing homeward. Our hearts rattled in our chests like rocks on the mountain, its granite outline glazed by the rising moon. Faster and faster we spun, our feet whirling like pinwheels. We leapt stone walls, avoided cow pats and thistles, twisted ankles and continued, unable to stop, each one racing the dark and the others, determined to be the first one to set foot on the road.

And then we were there, the house anchored like a lit ship before us. We crossed the road, clattered up the porch steps without speaking. Our thoughts were on ice cream and the shape of our own beds, and my stepbrother was laughing. The screen door banged. Moths rippled in eddies behind us. We went in, moving from darkness into a strangely light world—as if it were a safe place that we entered. As if there were no memory of blood upon glass there.

Supplies

for Shirley

Because I believed my stepmother hated me,
because I sat alone in the school auditorium
the day all the sixth-grade mothers came
and watched a film called *Growing Up and Liking It*
with their girls, I didn't tell her anything
when *It* arrived for the first time,
but went straight from the bus to my room
and sat with my legs clenched
around the institutional-sized Kotex
the school nurse had safety-pinned
to my stained Carter's panties.

I assume you have supplies? she'd said,
yanking up the panties so hard it hurt.
I didn't, but lied, knowing it wasn't
a question by the way she avoided my eyes,
hoping I'd find an answer in the dog-eared
booklet with anatomical drawings,
pictures of pretty girls
with perfectly combed hair
going swimming or riding,
while cheery captions urged me to
Remember, you can do all the things you usually do!

I had no supplies.
No quilted pink box like the one
my friend Caroline showed me,
tucked in a drawer with her mother's brassieres,

the little pads stacked, neat and white
as piles of linen, tampons in crackling paper
(*for when I'm older*, she whispered,
touching them with a reverent hand),
and the stretchy, lace-trimmed belts
in different colors like ads I had seen
in *Tiger Beat* for Frederick's of Hollywood.

I'd done my reading, but I wasn't prepared.
And so I sat in my room, aching, while the bright
arterial red turned a deep rust that smelled
smoky and strange, alive and dead
at the same time. I prayed it would end.
But it kept on flowing, no matter what I did,
until I went to her, desperation
winning out against fear.

And though those years together
were mostly about what didn't work,
I can't forget the plain white belt
she took from her dresser and slid
around my hips, adjusting a clean napkin
until it fit me exactly right,
and how she kissed me then, hard,
in the middle of the forehead,
and explained how to soak
bloodstains out in cold water.

Radio Love Poem

It's not true that I had nothing on. I had the radio on.
                    —Marilyn Monroe, in *Time* magazine, 1952

The radio makes me nervous. But there was a time when I loved it, thirteen and falling asleep to the hum of my black-cased transistor, its leather handle looped securely around one wrist. Pulse beat against pulse beat, I rocked on the radio's currents, adjusting my moods to the waves of the music, the deejays' announcements and even the commercials for "Su-n-n-days at Raceway Park!"

Murray the K, with his "Swinging Soirée." Wise Roscoe. And Alison Steele, "The Night Bird" with my own name, who came on at eleven, her voice of honey filtered over gravel as deliberately sexy as the new fires catching hold in my body. I knew them all on an intimate basis. I invited them into my room with a flick of one finger—voices that seduced from sixty miles away, downriver in New York City, brimming with secret knowledge about the meaning of my world.

Summer afternoons, the radio was girlfriend and boyfriend, dangling by its strap from the handlebar of my old Schwinn as I pedaled five miles out to clear, gray Lake Mamanasco, music drifting behind me. Baring my pale skin to the flat, white sun, I lay down, huddled alone on the striped bath towel I had imagined so Californian, feeling suddenly over-exposed in my homemade paisley bikini and waiting, just waiting, for the boys who swam and dove like schools of bright fish oblivious to my shy signals.

I smoked crumpled Tareytons. Stared, from behind *Jane Eyre,* into the water. Pretended to be interested in the abilities of Sun-In, Coppertone, and *Ingenue* to completely transform me. Turned that transistor up extra loud. "Red Rubber Ball," a ridiculous song played again and again, satisfyingly round with the promise of the worst being over, the morning sun rising, and everything turning out happily in the end.

I didn't even like the song. But I was the ball, bouncing along like an out-of-control dinghy on the force of those airwaves, a life preserver of music keeping me afloat while I bobbed to the raft, swimming with one arm, bearing the radio like torch or trophy above me, then rested on gray boards that smelled of algae and boat oil, before heading back to shore alone.

Radio love song. It wasn't even sound I craved, but protection against silence, the quiet places in my own head the ones I feared most because they named me as what I was, a lost station in search of an airway. The real world rushed in through a black plastic speaker, while I listened, captive to rhythms that were swirling inside me, and danced with myself in the hallway mirror, my fingers grooved in ridges from adjusting the painted silver dial.

But someone was always watching in that room that sparked bright with the energy of random electrical charges. In the middle of it all stood a girl looking for words she could say, hidden under the music, her brain crackling into life like sheets of summer lightning, or a thunderstorm breaking, or a transmitter beginning, finally, to send out signals, a first raw poetry she recognized as her own.

What the Body Knows

I was thirteen the December my stepbrother
Michael came home from boarding school
and decided he liked me more than before
(enough to experiment with at least), my body
transformed from knock-knees to lure. He
was all muscle and brain that holiday season,
stalking the house in tight black jeans,
quoting Sartre and Camus, playing Bob Dylan
on the hi-fi, and writing poems about death,
"the dark-winged avenger."

Barely past Nancy Drew, hooked on novels
with titles like *Wildfire at Midnight*,
I'd never seen anyone so slick, and the boys
I dreamed about at North Salem High School
dissolved to nothing fast—
even Peter Krinitsky, whose miniature
face I'd scissored from a blurry
soccer picture in the weekly *Bengal*
and hidden inside an imitation gold locket
whose chain left a green ring on my neck.

Crooning along with Rolling Stones songs,
giving each number emphasis with his hips,
Michael was as bad as Mick—
what we'd later call *wicked*,
though we didn't have that word yet.
I wondered how I could have ever thought
making JV cheerleading would be *it*,

the letters NS emblazoned on my chest
while I did cartwheels and the Tigers
lost another game to Peekskill or Pawling,
other little towns from nowhere like ours.

Michael knew about Baudelaire
and Kerouac and how to roll a joint.
I still faked inhaling cigarettes, and kept
a pink gingham-covered diary with a red felt heart
on its front, slit with a place for the pen I used
to praise Joe D'Entroni, who'd played in the band
they had for us the last night at 4-H camp
and kissed me afterwards, though I kept my teeth
clenched tightly in case he got fresh.

I might have even once believed
this was how girls got pregnant
and had to leave town, but whatever I believed
went out the window when Michael snake-
danced through the house, chugged milk
straight from the bottle, said, "Come here,
little Sis." "I'm not your Sis," I said,

but went anyway, my muscles
bent to his in a way
that made me think maybe
I loved this person I hated,
this brother who wasn't a brother, this boy-man
who pushed me up against the rose-patterned
wallpaper and ground into me with hips

that were so eager I would like to say
there was something good about it,
that our bodies spoke kindly to one another,
doing what the body knows to do, in the brief
moment before we felt my stepmother's
hands on our shoulders, pulling us apart—
back into the world where pain
opened its petals in time-lapse,
like a red flower pressed for years
inside the family Bible.

Stealing Clothes From My Stepmother

It wasn't fashion, but you
I wanted, all those times
when I crept,
a thief at fifteen,
into the sweet, steamy
heat of your
dressing room closet.

It was to be like you
that I tried all your clothes on,
slipping the silk camisole
with its French lace
over my skin, magic
that could transform me—
the "daughter"
who was not
your daughter—
into something other
than what I was.

It was to get close to you,
that I sneaked a suede jackets
out for the evening—
dancing to Jefferson Airplane
at the Capitol Theater—
or "borrowed" a satin-piped blouse
and returned it the next day,
the half moons of alien sweat
beneath each armpit a sure
guarantee of my capture.

There is no escape.
Beauty is what you gave me.
And I wanted to *be* you,
in your Villager twin sets
and crêpe de Chine sheaths,
a cloud of Estee Lauder
drifting behind you
like the scent
of a secret country.

But you would never have
guessed this from the way
we stood screaming,
the simple fact
of our competition
stretched between us,
real as my smart backtalk
or the hand you raised
to slap me with but dropped,
my face burning

with what lay, unspoken
under all my forays
through your most private
possessions. What you
might have accepted,
what I might have understood,

if I had been your blood daughter.
If I had known you loved me.

Along the Path

for my sister and brothers

The flowers that grow here by daylight are sleeping. They do not see us as we pass, our Eveready flashlights flickering great arcs into the forest. They do not stir as we trudge, laden with bedrolls and pillows, peanut butter sandwiches in wax paper, a wind-up alarm clock, and a kitchen-sized box of Ohio Blue Tip matches—provisions of a lifetime we carry, stuffed in Dad's old army rucksack.

The flowers do not hear us as we speak, our voices lowered to whispers that ripple outward in small puffs through the chill air and then vanish, moonlit on clear nights. Cloistered like dreams in an alcove of tall weeds, the flowers greet us in silence. Each bloom hangs suspended, a study in charcoal. No pigment, just shadows and fine lines. Pencil drawings. Engravings. Gradations of meaning we are too young to grasp.

In this dark, all color is secret, a message we ignore as we dash past in a small herd, intent on the hearth we have made among pine trees, eager to leave this wide space where dewy tendrils reach toward our bare legs from the grass.

But because I dally behind, because I am no longer afraid of the dark, I pause, alone at the line where the trees meet the edge of the meadow. Looking back down the still path, I want to ask, *Why is it we rushed so?* And: *What were we thinking?* It is only when held in the hand that the flowers will reach us. It is only when touched with the skin that memory lingers, unfolding through the dark, so that one says (even years later), *Ah, yes. It was summer. I was sixteen. Ah, yes. White heather, Indian paintbrush, common speedwell, meadow rue.*

Smoke

I knew about your reputation
before I knew you, heard how you'd stagger—
drunk off your ass at a keg party—
into a car with the boys' basketball team
and go down on every one. I'd seen them
dump you off afterwards, shoving you
out the door with their empty Budweiser bottles
and ashtrays of Marlboro butts.

But I needed to know you
and you knew to reach for me,
and the night I stepped forward
when you stumbled and fell from the car
became the two of us laughing each day
over cigarettes in the girl's room
before the bell sent us running—
you to Voc Tech Cosmetology,
me to Honors French.

You sewed me an Indian print dress
drenched with sandalwood and patchouli.
We skipped out of school, hitchhiked,
ripped off mirror dresses and albums,
and danced together in the bathroom
at the Om coffee house, the faint blue smoke
of our first joints swirling around us like silk.

I thought we told one another everything.

But what I remember now
is how you begged me to sleep over,
even on school nights.
And how we lay beside one another
in your French Provincial bed,
listening to your father
walk back and forth outside your door.
I feel better when you're here, you said once,
sinking into sleep like a child
while I stared at your collection
of "Dolls from Around the World"
and they stared back at me

the way they must have stared at him
when he came into your room
and put those hands that sliced
through sides of beef each day
upon you and made you do it.
Until you got it right. Until
it was what you knew how to do best.
Until there was no going back
from the boys in the car,
or your job as a call girl in Denver.

And God forgive me, Amanda.
I never even tried to phone,
or meet you for a drink
the way we used to meet
for cigarettes in the girl's room,
my fingers brushing yours,
all the things we never said
laid out on the table between us,

smoke still rising
through the bright blonde
garden of your hair.

Seventeenth Summer

Long after we went to bed, my sister and I'd lie awake, listening to the sound of my father arguing with my stepmother about her affair with his friend in the pharmaceutical business. They spoke softly at first but got gradually louder, his voice rubbing back and forth against her voice like a stick dragged across wood until the whole thing began smoking and they went at it in earnest, their words magnified for us by the network of makeshift heating vents tunneled through our two-hundred year old house.

And though we got high nearly every night, played John Mayall's *Bluesbreakers* over and over, and sometimes slept with our heads under our pillows—the muffle of feathers pressed like hands across our mouths —nothing we did could shut out the sound of their voices or the way they struggled together, his questions slamming into her taunts into the tears we pushed down our throats, swallowing them as if those two had entered our bodies, forcing their sorrow and rage upon us

until we burned with them, turning straight into the flames the way panicked horses will, confusing fire with safety or love that consumes what it touches, bright lesson that will not go out, no matter how much water I carry or how often I douse my memories of that house—where we were girls together, Jenny, where we kept each other company in the dark, growing up somehow, getting out . . . though you tell me now you cannot remember anything about it.

High School Boyfriends

Because they were willing to like me a little,
because they were willing to drape the heavy
animal warmth of their arms over my shoulders,
or hold me tight during slow dances
when the lights went down in the gym,
because they were willing
to claim me, like a new world,
or a wilderness waiting
green beyond the waves, I

let them do whatever they wanted,
my breasts rubbed raw
under the flint
of their fingers,
my hand cramped
from jerking off the cock
of Lee, Randy, John, Richard, Robert, Frank, and Jim,
each of them the same
hard, groping boy-shape
that bruised my lips
in backseat, field, or at
forbidden forest camp-outs,
then left me lonely, my fingers sticky
with the salt-wet slick of their come.

I didn't know any better,
I say to myself now.
I didn't know how to say no
and push their hands away.
But the body doesn't lie.

The body remembers forever.
And sometimes the ghosts
of boys' hands still smolder inside me,
a fire gone underground
where something green once grew.

Open Sesame

for Peter

In a B movie made the year
I was born, Tony Curtis plays
the great magician Harry Houdini.
My brothers and sister and I
must have watched it a dozen times,
mesmerized that snowbound week WPIX
played it twenty-four hours a day
on "Million Dollar Movie."

Hungry for spells and hocus-pocus
we swallowed it all, wanting to believe
that if rabbits and white doves could be pulled
from top hats and loose black sleeves,
there was a way out of anything,
even that house with its picket fence
where my father and stepmother
shouted each night,
then slept in separate rooms.

Nothing is what it seems.
But Houdini's escape from the steel trunk
dropped into the frozen Detroit River
is the scene that really sticks.

We watch it happen over and over:
the grappling hook breaks. The trunk,
nailed shut and lined with lead, plunges
through the ice. Houdini wriggles
from his handcuffs and shimmers through the wood.

The TV washes our faces with its blue glow.
And we are there with him, gasping for breath,
panting in air pockets, then emerging
triumphant through the ice,
knowing that nothing can hold us.

And afterwards, when the screen turns
to snow and escape is forgotten, Peter
goes from front door to back door, checking
and rechecking, making sure each catch
holds firm, locking us in for the night,
maintaining the illusion that we are protected
in that place we all want to get out of—
that locked safe, that whale's belly,
that steamer trunk lined with lead
only magic will open.

Lantern

for Steve

It was the year my father kicked my brother out of the house because my stepmother had goaded him until he broke—calling him *useless and good-for-nothing* until he snatched up a kitchen knife and held it at her throat. It was the winter he lived in the cottage in the woods, nothing but an old Boy Scout sleeping bag and an electric space heater to keep him warm. It was the December he found an old milking lantern in the barn and restored it, thinking whatever a fifteen-year-old boy forced from home thinks, hope of some kind hammering in his chest like a broken fist.

He sanded the lantern down to bare metal with steel wool, then polished it till it gleamed, ready for the black enamel he painted on, stroke by shining stroke, until it seemed new and beautiful enough to give my stepmother for Christmas. Who, when he handed her the package, knew exactly what to do, electrifying the lantern, installing it as the front porch light on that two hundred-year-old house where everyone in our family but my brother lived, where we quickly learned to find the switch in the dark.

So that, when I flick on the porch light at my own house in winter, I think of the two of them standing out there together, saying whatever it was they said that made things better but still not right, the lantern suspended between them, light passing from his hands into hers.

Eggs

for Steve, again

Halfway through his annual phone call
to apologize for missing my birthday,
my brother's voice changes.
He asks if I remember how the corgi mutts
brought in pheasant eggs when we were kids,
and how they held them—sometimes two at a time—
so gently they never once broke.

I remember the buff-olive eggs Megan
and Tina nudged from grass-lined nests.
And how they dropped the warm, slippery
treasures into our hands. My mother
always tucked them beneath a hen, just in case.
They never hatched, but lay there, lifeless
as the wooden egg used to stimulate laying.

My brother says,
They hatched, didn't they?
Don't you remember pheasant chicks
running around in the way-back coop?
I want to tell him, *Yes, they hatched.*
Every last one. There were pheasant chicks
running all over the place.

I want to give him the whole
bright yolk of his story
because it could have happened the way
he remembers and in memory it did, making
his voice familiar again, not a tense stranger's.

Because even if it isn't true
it tells more than he knows

about the gentle dogs
and the fields of our childhood,
and the small boy who stood there,
his buzz-cut as plush as the stuffed
alligator he held by one leg, watching
the pheasant chicks scurry before him,
bits of tawny fluff from a time
before everything broke.

In a Field, with Horses, 1972

The horses didn't belong to us, but because we boarded them it was easy, my first summer home from college, to pretend they were ours—the mare that shone like polished oak, the charcoal gelding, and the Appaloosa pony with one bad eye our neighbors bought for their children. Old, gentle, past the jumbled contradictions of time, the horses were rarely ridden, but just there, tails swishing like raw silk as they cropped alfalfa or took the tart apples from a hundred-year-old orchard we offered to them on outstretched hands.

During the day, the horses seemed to float, nearly motionless beneath maples or shimmering in clouds of dust and heat, each step executed with a purposeful slowness that caught at the place where words struggled in my throat. At night my sister and I could hear them snuffle and nicker near our window, drifting closer and closer like dreams of horses beside us, listening intently for something just beyond knowing in the enormous summer dark.

Once, I went outside and stood among them in my translucent white nightgown, my arm laced over the mare's broad back. I don't know what I hoped to accomplish, or why it was I couldn't sleep. But pressing my face into the mare's tangled mane soothed me as I stood, straining at the limits of family, in our shabby summer yard, my body washed with moonlight, my arms around that old horse who wasn't even mine, leaning into her side because it was firm and real, because I belonged there, and that belonging made me real too, as briefly, as keenly as the girl I was leaving behind.

My Stepmother's Ambrosia

for Shirley

Three times already this holiday season I've made my stepmother's ambrosia, stirring the coconut, pineapple, mandarin oranges, and miniature marshmallows into sour cream the way she did for parties when I was a girl. It isn't the healthiest treat, falling dangerously close to Jell-O molds or what a friend from the South calls "congealed salads," but everyone loves it. And they always laugh when I tell them it's my stepmother's ambrosia, so be careful: it's sweet, but with no nutritional value.

But that isn't true, or why would I carry the battered recipe card with me nearly twenty years now, the instructions written in her round hand so oddly like my own? People are different when you meet them again. And though the child's heart may not believe it, people change. So that in the middle of my life and late in hers, Shirley has become the mother I wanted, old hurts laid away like clothes I've long outgrown, the girl and the woman who screamed *You're not my mother* and *I'm glad you're not my daughter* not forgotten exactly, but forgiven for what they didn't know. She was my stepmother just six months after my mother died. And I was too scared to tell her that all I wanted was love, thick and sweet as the spoonfuls of ambrosia I'd sneak from the fridge before every party.

She ripped a shirt off my back once. I stole and wrecked her clothes. It never occurred to us that this might be normal, or that in the end the legacy is sweeter for being unexpected. My stepmother was never an inspired cook, and neither am I, preferring like her to stick my nose in the next new book. And though I remember my own mother's canned beans, pot roast, cherry pie, I don't have a single recipe of hers. What I have is this, a stained card with instructions for ambrosia—add one cup of everything, mix together, chill till the flavors blend. And when I tell Shirley how often I've made it this week, she sighs. *Oh, I got that recipe from my mother, when I was a girl.*

III.

The Blue Dress

My Parents' Dance Lessons, 1945

In the story my aunt tells,
this is how they met. It's
September, the war just over,
the air crisp as the creases
in my father's khaki pants,
bright as his Bronze Star,
pungent as the marigold
my mother tucks behind one ear,
the night they both sign
up for dance lessons
"the Arthur Murray way"
at the Statler Hotel
in downtown Philly.

He's there to meet girls, of that
I am certain, and she's there
for romance, though I don't think
that's what she would say,
both of them looking for something
as intangible as the cigarette smoke
that rises in old, deckle-edged photos—
everyone tough, glamorous, vampy.

Perhaps there are dance cards?
Or maybe partners are assigned?
The truth is, no one really knows
about the moment when their glance
catches and snags across the room,
a fishline pulling taut as they
place their feet on Murray's

famous "magic footsteps," and start
the slow luxury of reeling one another in.
Music spills from a scratchy
Victrola as she places her hand
on his shoulder, feels the slight
pressure of his palm against her back,
and they begin to move together,
her hesitant steps following
his over-enthusiastic swings,
until they are both lost in
"The More I See You" or "I Don't
Want to Walk Without You Baby,"
the future stretching out before them
like a polished oak dance floor.

I don't know if they went back
for more lessons, or how they learned
to dip and twirl and slide together,
though I once saw my father spin
my mother completely around—her skirt
flaring out around her like the bell
of a silk lamp shade—just months
before she died. It's their story
after all, the one with a secret
hidden deep inside it like all
love stories—bigger than we
are or will ever be—music
from a Big Band coming up
in the background, playing
"You'd Be So Nice to Come Home To,"
while our parents swoop and glide
in the spotlight, keeping back
just enough of the story to make us wonder.

Fever of Unknown Origin, 1955

At age two I nearly died, a fever of unknown origin sweeping me on dark swells while you floated, constant at my side. For six weeks you hovered, a blurred figure in a white gown with blue flowers, who leaned into my crib, crooning old songs I have never forgotten and praying, willing me into life again.

There was the touch of your hand on my cheek when they changed the i.v. in my ankle. And there was the knowledge that you slept beside me at night, a tall, blonde woman curled uncomfortably into the small cot at my side. Once I saw you leaning toward the window at twilight, staring into a sky starred gold by city lights. I thought I was dreaming, but you turned slowly, weeping, and somehow I realized, *She will be sad if I leave her. I must get better. I must come back from wherever I am.*

Years later, in the middle of Beethoven's Sixth Symphony, outdoors at the Hollywood Bowl, that same night sky opens above me and I hear you calling across time, across distance. *Come back, little girl,* you say. *Come back, my darling. Don't die. Please come back.* The wind lifts my hair, though the trees are not moving. In my adult life, sitting beside a man I love, I am three thousand miles from the place I last saw you, a woman walking out an arched door toward her own death in winter, white flakes swirling like an omen in her face.

It's summer, and I am far away. But your clear voice stretches like a rope from the land of the dead into the land of the living. It brings me back to the world, the way you brought me back as a sick child, the way you remind me to come back when I'm most tempted to give up and enter the kingdom of darkness. To come back because you are with me, though I'm no longer your little girl but a woman grown beyond you. To come back because you love me, because even half a lifetime later and one death between us, that is what remains.

Paradise

for Jenny and Steve

Memory believes before knowing remembers.
—William Faulkner

On the way back home to Wild Run Farm from the city, my brother and sister and I would fall asleep to the rhythm the wheels made, the Plymouth wagon we called "Gray Car" thrumming through the Pennsylvania dark. One minute my grandmother waved her handkerchief from her front porch in Germantown, and the next, the lights of Philadelphia winked out like fireflies behind us. In the back seat, Jenny and Steve made pillows of my mother's thighs. Up front, I lay down on the seat beside my father, the blue and gray upholstery pressing a grid into my cheek. I watched the long muscle of his khaki-covered thigh tighten, then relax, as he maneuvered the pedals.

The instrument panel glowed blue-green. I breathed in the scent of alfalfa and clover stretched out around us. My eyes opened and closed, opened and closed to the sound my parents' voices made, weaving together in the air above our heads like the two gold hands linked over the gold heart on my mother's ring. The car moved smoothly along, holding us in a swaying pocket of steadiness and light.

Then our driveway crunched beneath the wheels. We passed the grape arbor and pine trees, the mint patch, and the barn where the animals slept, each in its own bed of clean straw and starlight. We stopped near the back door where the porch light spilled a path toward us through the *breep . . . breep . . . breep* of crickets. My father carried my brother. My mother cradled my sister in her arms. Half asleep, I staggered between them. The oldest child, I held myself upright with a fistful of my mother's calico skirt, not yet knowing what it meant to step safely through the dark on a runner of bright gold, home a luminous door, always open before us.

Silver Shoes

The winter before you died
you bought a pair of silver
moiré pumps for parties. They shimmered
like moonlight on water when you walked,
spiked crescents gleaming
beneath the smoky plush of your coat.
But I wore them more than you,
teetering up and down the hall
for dress-up, my arches aching,
your empty rhinestone cigarette holder
flashing in my hand as I pretended to smoke
the Black Cats that Daddy brought you from Montreal.

When I slid my feet into your shoes
I was almost as tall as you,
their quiet sparkle like starlight
that sometimes salted my dreams.
And you knew to get me my own,
stopping at Wanamaker's on the way
into grandmother's and saying,
Pick whichever ones you want.

I chose a flower-spangled pair
that fit perfectly in a ladies five,
their sheen caressing my feet
the way canoes are held by water.
And when my older cousins teased me,
trying the pumps on, asking
could they keep them,

you said, *No, they're Abby's.*
She needs them for something.

You never said what for.
But when we got home I asked
if I could try the shoes on
one more time before I went to bed.
You slipped them onto my feet.
I wobbled, a little more certain,
out across the pool of blue braided rug.
The room was nearly dark.
I could not see your face
or guess what you saw
when you looked toward mine,
as I walked away from you
into the shadows, light
sparking out around me
with every step I took.

Raising Water

Solid and red as a mechanical heart, the hand pump stood, a British soldier at attention. Sentry of the back steps. Guardian of all the secrets hidden in our Pennsylvania yard.

It fascinated me, that scarlet presence out of another century. Cool to the touch, warming in sunlight, its trough of silver gushed up and outward like a river from beneath the land.

Each spring when the rains came, the pump ran, its handle open, the force of deep currents moving on their own. One year it paused that way in a hard frost—motion and the memory of motion caught as a cascade of silver arching toward the frozen ground.

And summers I stood, minutes at a time, pumping as if everything depended on the spill of clear water. How my arms ached within their sockets. How the blisters stood out in little bubbles, fierce red spots burning in my palms.

I felt like an adult, but couldn't have said why. I loved the sound of water falling, and the way it glistened, a sheet of silver fabric draped across the steps. I loved the wetness. The pansies drinking. The strange salt taste of sweat upon my lip.

I didn't know I loved the work, the fear, the rhythm. The effort of all things dark and secret—pulled, with the sparkle of clear water, from deep beneath the ground. I knew only that I loved pumping, and that when I had pumped long enough and hard enough, the handle would move for a few strokes under its own power. I would bend then, my hands cupped into a small bowl beneath the shimmer. And lifting, I would drink and drink again.

I didn't know what I raised, a girl alone at a red pump, playing. But how often I think of it since, feeling again the ache in my shoulders. The creak of old metal pulling up secrets. And the cold, cold water, its message an urgent language, burning in my palms.

My Mother's Pastels

My mother's pastels came in a thin, green box from France that slid open, its slotted drawer filled with sticks of solid color that looked good enough to eat, words like fuchsia, chartreuse, bleu celeste printed on their tattered wrappers, names of colors I had never imagined. *Toutes les nuances du spectre solaire* it said on the label. "All the colors of the rainbow," my mother translated, her voice filling with light the way her face did when she held a pastel in her hand.

Mostly I just looked, but sometimes I tried them out, trading my fat Crayolas and stubby pencils for those wands of pigment and light that grabbed at the page and dusted my fingers with grains of color like pollen. I sat close beside her, moving my hand over the sketchbook the way she did, trying to copy every angle and gesture, pictures of trees flowing from my fingers like water, my mother's translation naming the shivery feeling that came when the world outside fell away and there was nothing but color between me and the page.

She never kept her sketches, but I felt them sometimes, forming out there in a place just beyond her gaze as she plucked chickens, put up tomatoes, bent to put winter chains on the rusty Plymouth wagon that ferried us to school. I don't know exactly what she saw, only the colors she gave me, my hands filled with possibilities for every single page.

Which is why I keep her pastels in my desk drawer, to remind myself how many colors there are in a life, shading in a bright band from red at one end to violet at the other. *Toutes les nuances du spectre solaire.* All the variations of sunlight filtered through the prism of rain. My mother the artist. My mother the 1950s mom. My mother a woman I will never know, mute and mysterious as the snapshot of her sketching in college, a pastel raised in mid-stroke, the drawing board balanced on her lap like a child.

Signing My Name

An artist always signs her name,
my mother said when I brought her my picture,
a puddled blur of scarlet tempera
I thought resembled a horse.

She dipped the brush for me
and watched while I stroked my name,
each letter drying, ruddy,
permanent as blood.

Later, she found an old gilt frame
for me at an auction.
At my request we repainted it pink,
encasing the wobble-headed horse I'd conjured
as carefully as if it were by da Vinci,
whose notebooks on art
she was reading that summer.

Even when I was six, my mother
believed in my powers, her own unsigned
pencil sketches of oaks and sugar maples
flying off the pad and disappearing
while her French pastels hardened,
brittle as bone in their box.

Which is why, when I sign my name,
I think of my mother—all she couldn't say
burning in primary colors—
the great red horse I painted
still watching over us,
the way it did those first years
from the sunlit wall of our kitchen.

Balancing

for my father

That first October in town,
when the doctors told my father
that my mother was dying,
he taught me how to stay upright

on a bicycle. Each evening after work,
he'd clench his pipe between his teeth
and run along behind me in shirtsleeves,
a blur of sparks and whiteness—when I
looked back—one hand just touching
the fender of my shiny, three-speed Schwinn.

Keep pedaling! he'd shout as I wobbled forward,
hesitant on those impossibly thin wheels,
knuckles white, arms stiff, legs surging until
I was the motion, my braids unraveling behind me
like ropes from another world. I did what my father said.
I kept pedaling, straight down Bellewood Avenue

into the darkness, the thrill of balancing
a steadiness that held me from within
as I peeled past familiar houses
with their tuna casseroles and pot pies,
then looped out further—
all wind-swish and goose bumps—
to where I'd never been,
not knowing when it was he let the fender go
and watched me disappear from him
through leaf shadow and black,

or how it was he knew to tell me
everything I'd need to know:
Keep pedaling. I've got you. Don't look back.

Each Broken Note Shining

The music lessons
were my mother's idea.
So I kept on practicing for the Winter Recital
after she left for the hospital,
pretending she was still there,
as she'd been the afternoon
we rented the violin in its black case
smelling of cherry-eucalyptus cough drops
and other children's hands.

I loved the faded purple velvet inside
that changed colors and caught at the light,
the honey-colored instrument scripted with S's
for sound, the silky chin-rest, and the bow—
a lance of gleaming horsehair I learned
to tighten, rubbing it rough
with a cake of rosin that sprinkled
my body with powdery stars.

All that autumn I had a purpose,
carrying the violin back and forth from school—
the case banging against my knees or bumping
across the handlebars of the black Schwinn
she'd given me for my birthday—
as it got dark earlier, and snow fell
in a scatter of silver,
and the fourth graders struggled
to master "Twinkle, Twinkle, Little Star."

But on Recital night,
I saw only my father, blur
of his tired face far back in a middle row.
And me, wearing a plaid madras dress
too thin for the season, stretched-out
kneesocks sliding into my Buster Browns,
my body tense and resonant as the instrument

I dragged the bow across,
each broken note shining
as I stood there, playing
what I couldn't say to my father.
My foot tapped in time
to that screech of grief,
that starless sky, that lullaby
so transfigured.

The Blue Dress

Three months before her death, my father
bought my mother a blue dress at Altman's.
It was a simple shirtwaist,
polished cotton that looked
like a garden at midnight,
sprigs of white and yellow flowers
blooming against a dark blue field.
Tiny ruffles cascaded down the placket,
covering the flat, scarred places
where her breasts had been.

It was the first new dress
she'd had in years besides homemade
clothes she'd sewn from remnants,
and she twirled in it before her children,
blushing, laughing, suddenly a girl again,
the full skirt belling out around her
like Ginger Rogers'
when she danced with Fred Astaire.

It was too late, of course,
though she wore the dress each day
that autumn as if the feel
of it against her body
was like my father's hands.
Still, I love them for buying
that blue dress together.

And when my aunt
said the blue was too dark
to be buried in,
my father insisted,
holding the dress in his arms
the way he'd held my dancing mother,
all the things he couldn't do to save her
wrapped, in a scattering of flowers,
across a dark blue field.

Last Photograph of My Family

It was November, 1962, when we posed for the picture—formal, black and white—at Agnes Bello's House of Portraits, down the street from the Dobbs Ferry Free Library (where I went every weekend, looking for yet another volume of *Lives of Remarkable Women*). What I remember is sun on the way in, and a stiff wind off the Hudson. How the light shone before we entered the building. And the way the door shut off color behind us, though I could swear we stepped through red velvet drapes as we moved toward Agnes herself, dressed all in black, spikes of white hair sticking out around her head.

The picture was my parents' idea, but Agnes posed us, seeing whatever it is photographers see, and arranging us around my mother like small planets, or a modern Madonna and family—mother as center of the world. In the photograph, my father and I sit on her right side, my brother and sister on her left. I sit sidesaddle between my parents, my body turned toward hers. Her hair, gone gray from illness, curves around her face in waves and curls she set last night with pins.

"Say cheese!" Agnes Bello says, and we all smile. Only my mother knows she will die. My father has heard the words, but cannot believe them. In a few weeks he will drive her to Cleveland, where the last treatment will fail. And we kids? We sit carefully around the edge of my mother's secret, protecting it the way one protects something one knows but does not know. In the monochromatic world of the photograph, her blue dress is black. Only the flowers shine, faintly white on its dark fabric, dozens of stars falling into deep water.

No matter how many times I look at the photo, it is still six weeks before she dies. My mother's lips curve in a smile that isn't a smile exactly, but what a smile knows it will be in memory, something smudged, fading even as everyone swears to remember. My mother sits there, gazing straight ahead, the luminous gray eyes she has passed down to my sister looking beyond us—past the camera, past Agnes Bello under the black cloth—to the world outside the picture, that shoreline only the dead can see.

A Child's Book of Death

I don't know who watched over your body, Mother, after you'd left it, or how my father got you from Cleveland to Dobbs Ferry. I only know that you arrived, motionless and as chill to the touch as the flesh of certain poisonous mushrooms. I was afraid of you then—though it seemed disloyal—and thought maybe I'd killed you, praying for you to die when you did not return as you'd promised.

Night after night, kneeling beside the spool bed, my pink flannel nightie with lambs tucked around my ankles, the floor breathing snaky drafts, the sisal carpet pricking my knees, I begged the great and implacable dark to make you better and bring you home, offering up Babar or Barbie the way I'd offered Raggedy Ann, on whom I operated, slitting her kapok-filled chest with nail scissors and digging my fingers in deep for her heart.

Which was supposed to be real, the way you were but then were not, as you lay before us, your body stuffed with darkness I smelled but couldn't see, the distance you'd travelled as enormous as all the states that slept between us while you lay dying in your high, white hospital bed, and Jenny and Steve and I prayed for you—*Our Father who art in heaven . . . . Now I lay me down to sleep*—every prayer we knew, our words a useless gabble we wanted to be true, falling from the small, mint-scented churches of our mouths.

The Right Color

for Jenny

The day we buried my mother, my aunt said the dresses my sister and I picked out weren't dark enough for a funeral. The corduroy jumpers she'd sewed us before she went away—one sky-blue, the other slate—were all wrong, Aunt Betty said as she reached into the closet, looking for something suitably somber. And besides, she added, they were home-made. Didn't we want to look our best?

We did. But the day my mother had bought the fabric, she'd let us choose whatever we wanted, the ribbed plush changing colors as we rubbed our fingers against the shining nap. And she'd fitted the pieces of pinked cloth right to our bodies—a dart here, a tuck there—making the jumpers ours in a way no store-bought dresses could ever be. So we put them on, buttoning each other into the garments she had stitched for us on the old black Singer.

Then I licked the tip of my index finger and smoothed out Jenny's eyebrows the way my mother used to do. We were getting dressed up. We were going somewhere important. We were making ourselves as perfect and beautiful as we knew how to be, clad in the blue corduroy jumpers she'd made, dressed in exactly the right color to kiss her good-bye, as we bent toward her through the sweet stink of lilies.

My Mother's Clothes

After the party
that came after the funeral,
when the last neighbors had gone home
with their sympathy, empty casserole

dishes, and promises to call soon,
my father asked her sisters
if they wanted my mother's clothes.
He stood in the bedroom

and threw the closet door open,
pulling out her fake fur coat
with the rose satin lining,
the pair of silver party shoes

she'd worn twice, and a row
of homemade dresses she'd sewn,
rick-rack decorations zigzagging
around the collars and sleeves.

My aunts stepped back as if
he'd struck them, or they could
catch cancer from touching
what once touched her.

And the more
my father pressed upon them,
the more firmly they refused, until
I wanted to hurl myself at their feet

and beg them to take something
even if they only threw it away
when they got home. Anything
to stop my father standing there,

her dresses draped in his arms
the way she was in the photograph
of them crossing the threshold.
But all I could do was stand

in the closet later for hours,
shutting the door, and wrapping
myself in the shape and scent
of what remained of her,

until I slept,
and my father found me,
curled under the fur coat
with the rose satin lining,

my cheek pillowed against
the sparkling shoes
he took to Goodwill
early the next day.

Madame Alexander's "Amy"

Two weeks after my mother's death, the doll was waiting under the tree, the blonde-haired Amy I'd dreamed over in the Sears Christmas catalog, running my finger over the small photograph as if it would help me see her more clearly, reading her description over and over, the wish book consulted so often it fell open at the page where she sat with her sisters from *Little Women* as if the four of them were waiting for tea.

She was the artist I wanted to be. And so I put her name at the top of the list we mailed my mother at the hospital, never doubting her ability to grant wishes or make dreams real. It had to have been my father who bought her, but I couldn't figure out how my mother wrote the tag signed with her name, just that the doll was there that first Christmas morning without her, new-doll-smell clinging to my hand as I lifted Amy from her wrappings in wonder and fear, her hair pulled up with a black velvet ribbon, a white organdy pinafore spilled over her blue dress like clouds.

I wanted to love her, and in some way I did, though I was afraid of her too, unsure exactly where she had come from, so cold and hard and unalive in my arms, with sapphire eyes that clicked open and shut, a doll that stared up at me from among blue paper printed with stars; a doll I couldn't ever really play with, worried I'd muss her with the grit of my life; a doll I once planned to bury in the backyard, and who watched while I was unable to do it; a doll who came like an emissary from the country of death to tell me that childhood was over, and she was the last plaything;

a doll I still have, sitting high on a shelf in the room where I write, her rosebud mouth clamped shut around the mystery of how my dead mother got her to me, her blonde curls forever tight and unplayed with, one plastic foot bare, still missing a patent leather shoe.

First Haircut, 1963

After my mother died
my long hair became a problem.
My aunts braided it at first,
their hands so much like her hands
I had to look away from myself in the mirror.

Then there was only my father,
his fingers tangled like splinters in silk.
I tried to teach him what I didn't know myself—
Over and under, Daddy; I think you go over and under—
my head bowed so he couldn't see how it hurt.

No matter what I did, I couldn't help out,
or show him how she'd bound the tea-colored
strands that sparked stars into glossy ropes
and made me who I was—the girl with long braids
that flew out behind her in streamers when she ran.

Most of all, I couldn't lean into his body
while he braided, my body swaying with each stroke
the way it had with hers. Which was why I agreed
when he said, *I'm sorry, honey. I can't get the hang of it.*
I think we're going to have to get it cut.

I've never forgotten the kiss of steel
that left me lightheaded, the air cold against my nape,
aware I wasn't Rapunzel or Jo March or even Tressy
whose short hair grew when you pressed on her stomach,
but a girl in mourning, carrying lopped-off braids home

in a blue net bag to put away in a secret place, deep
in the bottom drawer of the mirrored, mahogany dresser
I'd stood before every morning, watching her fingers fly
over and under, as she wove the waterfall tight and smooth,
the world she made there safe, shining, whole.

With No Words to Name This

I do not think my father meant wrong,
those first raw weeks after my mother's death,
when he took me, weeping,
into their bed, and held me,
shaking, while the whole house slept,
wrapped in its navy blue blankets
of grief and exhaustion.

I think he meant well,
meant to soothe the way
my mother had, her soft, powder-
scented body curving around me
when I was sick or scared.
I cannot remember
if he pressed his face
to my flat chest,
where the nipples floated
hard as unripe grapes.

Or if he touched me
in that cleft of darkness,
my small black sea heaving
against the arch of pubic bone.
I do not even know if he held me
against his own hardness,
or if he only held me,
and what I almost remember
is a story I have invented
to explain away a dream,
my body a knot of wet rope
only a mother's hands
could untangle.

Black Stone

My first week back at school after the funeral
I found a black stone on the playground at recess.
I was walking alone while the other girls
played jump rope, the familiar rhymes
and slap of the rope against pavement
like a language I'd once known
but stopped speaking when Mrs. Carter
made me stand at my desk
and told the whole fourth grade
to *Give Alison a warm welcome back,*
and tell her how sorry we were
to hear about her mother.

The stone shone out at me from among
faded candy wrappers and old leaves.
I picked it up because it was different
and gave me something to hold onto, perfect
black oval so smooth and warm in my hand.
After that, I carried it everywhere,
deep in the linty cave of my pocket,
or placed carefully under my pillow
where I could reach out and touch it at night.
Once or twice I even held the stone in my mouth,
balancing it on my tongue like petrified music,
wondering what would happen to me if I swallowed.

I planned to have it drilled
or fitted to hang on a gold chain,
like a picture of a locket I'd seen
in a tattered copy of *Godey's Ladies Book*

my mother had found at an auction.
I didn't know then about mourning brooches
or jet cameos carved with faces of the dead.
I just liked rubbing the stone against my cheek,
and holding its slick darkness close to my heart.

I carried the stone all winter,
like a secret I knew so well
I slowly forgot what it meant.
Then one day, when I hadn't reached
to touch it for a while, it was gone.
And though I've looked many times
through books about rocks and minerals,
searching for its name, my stone is never there—

black lake, unblinking eye, lozenge of darkness
that stopped my crying when I held it,
cupped in my palm like a fossilized tear,
polishing its surface till it glowed
with the oil from my skin—
all the things I couldn't say
bound up in it, hard, black, durable,
permanent as death in my hand.

Small Planets

They came free with volumes of the *Golden Encyclopedia* my mother bought each week at the A&P. Hard-shelled, plastic replicas of planets my father punched from blue sheets, glued together in 3-D, and suspended on lengths of clear line that dissolved when night came, the whole solar system floating above us in indigo dreams.

The mobile glowed in the dark, lit by phosphorescent stars he'd dotted on its supports with a small brush, and I'd fall asleep watching it spin, each planet wobbling in updrafts and downdrafts, faithful to gravity and its place in the sun. I'd close my eyes and the planets were family, traveling among the fixed stars in a reliable pattern. I learned to name them that way—Mercury, Venus, Mars—revolving around the sun the way we all did around my mother.

I don't know what happened to the mobile after she got sick and we moved to town. Thrown away, perhaps, like so many things. Sometimes I dream I've found it, tangled at the bottom of a Mayflower packing box, the planets' hard shells dented. I untangle the lines and press the spheres my father called *wanderers* round again. Then I stand on a kitchen chair, and hang it up in the big bedroom where I sleep with my sister and brother while our parents are gone on that last trip to save her. It is winter and stars still glow outside, though their light is faint.

But no matter how hard I try—a girl on a red chair, trying to fix things—I can't make the mobile balance right. The planets spin, cock-eyed and crazy. I'm not tall enough to reach the sky, and the sun breaks apart in my palms, hollow as the *Golden Encyclopedia's* words about cancer. Nothing is what it seems. Planets, life, my mother. How a whole family plummets, off course, through the night. Why the starlight comes off in silver flecks on my hands.

Cape Ann Summer

After my mother's death we hunted sea stars
at low tide, reaching through the green water
at Annisquam to the algae-covered rocks.
We pried their suctioned grip loose
and piled them in the bottom of the boat
as if they'd shine for us the way our aunts'

faces did, tucking us in at night. Soft-bosomed aunts.
We clung to them at the beach, hands like sea stars,
until I understood that each body is a boat
capable of floating alone in salt water.
But inside me an impulse for death ran loose.
We laid out sea stars to dry on the rocks.

Something about grief was solid as rock,
a sharp secret I tried to hide from my aunts.
Each night in bed I let my bucket of tears loose.
Salt stung my face the way sun burned the sea stars.
Their arms went limp, then stiff without water.
Spiny ghosts floated past my window like lost boats

I'd read about, imagining how I'd take our rowboat
out and let go, wood slamming into splinters upon rock.
Everything we needed to know swirled there in the water.
My mother had planned for this with our aunts.
But no one stopped us from drowning the sea stars
in air. And though I slept with my long hair loose

on the familiar fancywork pillow, dreams loosed
me from my mooring like the old blue rowboat
run aground, into the sucking sound sea stars
make at low tide, each one plastered on its own wet rock.
Someone's fingers pried at me and I screamed for my aunt.
She knew the history of loss is written in water.

But I kept seeing my mother's face vanish in water.
No matter how hard I clung to her, my arms tore loose.
I whispered this to my lavender-scented aunt
who leaned across the candlewick spread in her boat-
necked gown, and encircled me with her arms, rocking
me to sleep again as we named aloud the stars

that tumbled with me into green water shadowed by the boat
where my mother drifted, fingers trailing, loose as seaweed above the rocks,
and my aunt held the bucket I couldn't stop filling with stars.

A Box of My Mother's Hair

My mother was a wonder at saving things, making do. Sewing scraps, dryer lint. Even the cat's fur was pulled from the brush and tossed to the wind so that birds might use it. But what to do with this box of her curls, clipped in 1932, when she was thirteen, and placed by my grandmother in a fold of pink tissue no one has opened till now?

I hold my breath when I lift the lid, afraid of mold, spiders, death, the ghost she has been for me since I was a girl, rising in a spiral of smoke like some sort of reverse genie, croaking *Look not upon these things; you will be trapped here if you do.*

But I have to look, the long blonde curls are so alive. They glisten in the sun, gold threads rippling when I lift them to the light that hasn't fallen on them in seventy years. The spirals loop around my fingers like punctuation to all my questions, sunlit waves the shape of a mermaid's tail.

I run them through my fingers until I can conjure the day my grandmother cut them. And how she must have watched the curls fall to the floor and been unable to throw them away, the unearthly radiance of each strand a kind of intimation.

I've seen a Victorian mourning brooch made of human hair. Could snap a few of these curls into a locket with my mother's likeness if I chose. But though every moment brings us closer to death, I know that hair isn't really alive. That it grows a half inch in the winter and twice that in summer. And it was my grandmother who told me it keeps on growing after we die, as if the body doesn't know how to stop doing what it knows to do.

I can't remember my mother's face exactly anymore, except from pictures. And so it's strange to hold a piece of her in my hand this way, like the knucklebone of a saint or a scrap of blue cloth clipped from the hem of the dress she was buried in. The body that bore me has been dust for over forty years.

Sometimes we save too much. And sometimes not enough. The moment my grandmother wanted to preserve is real as this slippery, silken skein. As my mother, who stands before her, on the farthest edge of girlhood, not even noticing when my grandmother lifts the curls from the floor and tucks them in tissue—this shimmering legacy I now touch and sniff and brush against my own cheek, as if it will tell me who my mother was. . .or what it means that I have so long outlived her.

Yellow October

In memory of my mother, and for Sue Wicks

Suddenly it comes to me
as I sit here in the late light
of yellow October, everything in the backyard
illuminated around me—

yellow the maple leaves,
yellow the columbine stalk
yellow the sunlight
falling across my shoulders
in wide gold bands—

that it was about this time
nearly thirty years ago
when you began making preparations
to leave us forever,
wrapping yourself a little more each day
into your old black coat
with the polished brass buttons.

When I was very young
you kept a vigil
beside my hospital crib
the spring my fever wouldn't come down
and the doctors told you
I would probably die.
No she won't, you said,
standing, sitting, sleeping beside me
until you were all I could see
and I felt your gaze upon me,

melting the ice they had packed me in
the way this yellow light
soaks into my shoulders.

I could not do the same for you,
calling you back from the frontier
that separates the dead from the living
the way a mother calls a child.
And yet I see now, in yellow October,
that it is not losing you that matters
so much as knowing you at all,

that you are the autumn
I pull around my shoulders each year
like a soft woolen shawl, grateful
for such a wide swath of yellow light
woven between the black borders.

Notes on the Poems

"Red," page *17* and "Baldy Notch, via Devil's Backbone," page *21*: Mt. Baldy, officially known as Mt. San Antonio, is *10,064* feet tall and the highest peak in Southern California's San Gabriel Mountains.

"Leaving Dorland Mountain," page *37*: Dorland Mountain is in the Palomar Range, southeast of Temecula, California.

"The Barbie Birthday," page *59*: Some of the information in this poem is from *The Barbie Chronicles*, edited by Yona Zeldis McDonough.

"Hunt Mountain," page *74*: At *980* feet, it is the highest point in North Salem, New York.

"Eggs," page *95*: Corgis are a sheepherding dog of Welsh origin.

Acknowledgments

Grateful acknowledgment is made to the editors of the following publications in which these poems or earlier versions of them appeared:

The American Literary Review: "Instinct"
Anemone: "Along the Path"
Ascent: "Daily"
Birmingham Poetry Review: "In Any Language"
Calapooya: "From One Life to the Next"
Crazyhorse: "A Bowl of Sugar"
Connecticut Review: "The Barbie Birthday"
5 A.M.: "A Child's Book of Death"
Frontiers: A Journal of Women's Studies: "My Mother's Clothes" and "My Life as a Horse" (under the title "Girlhorse")
Green Mountains Review: "Epilogue"
Kalliope: A Journal of Women's Literature and Art: "Black Stone" (Sue Saniel Elkind Prize)
Lifeboat: A Journal of Memoir: "Hunt Mountain" and "In a Field, with Horses, 1972"
Margie: The American Journal of Poetry: "Magic Eight" and "With No Words to Name This"
New Letters: "What the Body Knows"
Nimrod: "My Parents' Dance Lessons, 1945" and "Small Planets"
The North American Review: "Each Broken Note Shining," "My Mother's Pastels" and "First Haircut, 1963"
Petroglyph: "Looking at MRI Scans of My Brain"
Prairie Schooner: "The Blue Dress"
Puerto del Sol: "Eggs" (under the title "Halfway through His Annual Phone Call, My Brother Asks if I Remember")
Rattle: "No Matter How Much Sunlight"
Sing, Heavenly Muse!: "Raising Water" and "The Grief of Animals"

Southern Poetry Review: "Joan of Arc"
The Southern Review: "The Habit of Its Fit"
Sou'wester: "Ring-O-Levio" and "Relapse"
Spoon River Poetry Review: "Ordering Clothes from Victoria's Secret" and
        "Fever of Unknown Origin"
Tar River Poetry: "Balancing"

"Ring-O-Levio," "With No Words to Name This," "Supplies," "What
the Body Knows," "Smoke," "High School Boyfriends," "The Habit of
Its Fit," and "Ordering Clothes from Victoria's Secret" also appeared in
a chapbook, *What the Body Knows,* from Parallel Press (2002).

The following poems also appeared in anthologies and the editors are
gratefully acknowledged:
"Leaving Dorland Mountain" in *And a Deer's Ear, Eagle's Song, and Bear's
Grace* (Cleis Press); "Supplies" and "Smoke" in *Boomer Girls: Poems by
Women of the Baby Boom Generation* (University of Iowa Press); "Silver
Shoes" and "Signing My Name" in *Claiming the Spirit Within: A Sourcebook
of Women's Poetry* (Beacon Press); "Lifeline" in *Fruitflesh: Seeds of Inspiration
for Women Who Write* (Harper SanFrancisco); "Twelve Below Zero" in *The
Glacier Stopped Here* (Isthmus Publishing); "Spring Geography" in *Men and
Women: Together and Alone* (The Spirit That Moves Us Press); "My Ex-
Husband Asks Me Who Reads My Rough Drafts" in *The Party Train: A
Collection of North American Prose Poetry* (New Rivers Press); "Red" and
"Baldy Notch, Via Devil's Backbone" in *Poetry Loves Poetry* (Momentum
Press); "Stealing Clothes from My Stepmother" in *Women and Stepfamilies:
Voices of Anger and Love* (Temple University Press).

"Supplies" was also included in *The Greatness of Girls: Famous Women Talk
About Growing Up* (Andrews McMeel); "Calf Season" was also included
in *A Voice of One's Own* (A Room of One's Own Bookstore).

This book has been a long time in the making, and I offer warm thanks
to the many who helped along the way. The memory of my mother,
whose spirit animates so much of this collection. My father, my first

model of a writer and the one who helped me believe I could do it too. Helen Glyer, who helped me find my way back into the world of words at a critical juncture. All the women in Holly Prado Northup's Los Angeles workshops, where I found my voice. My friends and colleagues at the University of Wisconsin–Whitewater. David Glyer, for his many years as my first and most painstaking reader; a number of these poems would not have been possible without his support. Katherine Wells and Diane Carver, two-thirds of the *tres mujeres*. Deb Gillespie for poems, and friendship. Leslie Ullman, Mark Cox, Gail Mazur, Marilyn Nelson, Susan Mitchell, and especially Mark Doty—for everything at Vermont College and beyond. The memory of Bill Truesdale and New Rivers Press, for encouragement and belief in the work. The women in my private workshops for all they've taught me. Sharon Doubiago for her courage and example. Julia Weaver for our parallel journeys. Josie Avery, for the girls we were together. The women in both my Madison writing groups, muses and midwives all, with a special gratitude to Susan Elbe and Jesse Lee Kercheval for their discerning second read-throughs. My stepmother, Shirley Townsend, for her love and ability to transcend the past. My sister and brother, Jenny and Steve Townsend, and stepbrothers, Michael and Peter Wittreich, for the stories of our lives, though they might tell them differently. Susan Wicks, for poems back and forth across the Atlantic. Robert Alexander, for his support and fine editing; any remaining infelicities are mine. This book would not exist without him. Judith Sornberger, for the door standing open. Jackie Melvin, dearest *poetessa*, for twenty years of poems and friendship and for her meticulous proofreading. Richard Hunt, for his unflagging friendship, and all those Sunday night, long-distance phone calls, listening to the week's poem. Holly Prado Northup, deepest friend of the soul. And my husband, Tom Umhoefer, without whom all the words in the world would mean little.

I would also like to thank Cottages at Hedgebrook and Soapstone Women's Writing Retreat, where this book was begun and finished, for the blessing of time and nurture.

About the Author

———⟨⟨O⟩⟩———

Alison Townsend was born in Pennsburg, Pennsylvania and raised there and in North Salem, New York. She graduated from Marlboro College and received an MFA from Vermont College. She is the author of a previous collection, *What the Body Knows*, from Parallel Press. Her poetry and essays have appeared in many literary journals, including *The American Literary Review, Calyx, Crazyhorse, 5 AM, Kalliope, New Letters, Nimrod, The North American Review, Prairie Schooner, Puerto Del Sol, Rattle,* and *The Southern Review*. Her work has also been anthologized in collections such as *Are You Experienced?: Baby Bom Poets at Midlife, A Fierce Brightness: Twenty-five Years of Women's Poetry, Fruitflesh: Seeds of Inspiration for Women Who Write, The Greatness of Girls: Famous Women Talk about Growing Up, Intimate Kisses, Boomer Girls: Poems by Women of the Baby Boom Generation, Claiming the Spirit Within: A Sourcebook of Women's Poetry,* and *The Party Train: A Collection of North American Prose Poetry*. An Assistant Professor of English, Creative Writing, and Women's Studies at the University of Wisconsin-Whitewater, she also teaches In Our Own Voices, a private writing workshop for women. She lives with her husband, dog, and cats in the farm country outside Madison, Wisconsin·

Author photo by Tom Umhoefer

The Marie Alexander Poetry Series

Series Editor: Robert Alexander

Volume 6
The Blue Dress
Alison Townsend

Volume 5
Moments Without Names:
Morton Marcus

Volume 4
Whatever Shines
Kathleen McGookey

Volume 3
Northern Latitudes
Lawrence Millman

Volume 2
Your Sun, Manny
Marie Harris

Volume 1
Traffic
Jack Anderson